bryan
WHITE

bryan WHITE

country cool

grace catalano

LAUREL-LEAF BOOKS

Published by
Bantam Doubleday Dell Books for Young Readers
a division of
Random House, Inc.
1540 Broadway
New York, New York 10036

Visit us on the Web! www.randomhouse.com

Educators and librarians, for a variety of teaching tools, visit us at www.randomhouse.com/teachers

ISBN: 0-440-22826-3

RL: 6.4

Printed in the United States of America
April 1999
10 9 8 7 6 5 4 3 2 1
OPM

For my dad

ACKNOWLEDGMENTS

The author would like to thank Joseph Catalano and Rose Miele for their assistance in the preparation of this book. Thanks to Sam Alan, Phil Berry, and my mom, Rosemarie Catalano, for their endless support and encouragement. Thanks also to Grace Palazzo, Ralph J. Miele, Mary Michaels, and Jane Burns.

And special thanks to Beverly Horowitz, Lawrence David, and everyone who worked on this book at Random House.

CONTENTS

one

look at him now

bryan White is one of the new breed of performers in Nashville shaking things up in country music. In just five years, the country singing sensation has soared to fame by recording consistently high-quality material and remaining true to his roots. His boyish good looks and superb tenor voice have had legions of teenage girls screaming and swooning since the day he first burst onto the music scene.

Bryan's accomplishments are amazing. His first two albums, *Bryan White* and *Between Now and Forever,* were simultaneously certified platinum, selling more than one million copies each.

His third release, *The Right Place,* shipped to stores gold and is nearing the one million mark.

Bryan has racked up five number-one hit singles, toured with top names like Vince Gill, Diamond Rio, Patty Loveless, and LeAnn Rimes, and won a mantelful of awards. In 1996 he beat out LeAnn Rimes for the coveted CMA (Country Music Association) Horizon Award for most promising newcomer.

"That was an amazing night," he reveals. "I just feel that someday I can show my kids that award and say, 'Hey, this is the mark I made in country music history.' That will always be there."

Despite his super success, Bryan has remained incredibly down-to-earth. He has built a solid reputation as one of country music's true nice guys. And he did it just by being himself.

"I never try to be someone I'm not," he says. "And if I caught myself trying to do that, I'd immediately stop.

"There have been so many great qualities and morals handed down to me that I've grown up with over the years," Bryan continues. "It's like my grandmother has always said: 'Just treat people the way you want to be treated.' "

Bryan achieved his success *his* way. Country music's clean-cut, handsome heartthrob doesn't fit the stereotype of a country singer. He wears no hat, no cowboy boots, and no Wranglers. He won over thousands of fans with his heartfelt ballads and breezy country pop songs.

He is country music's first teen idol and is the kind of guy even mothers adore. He takes the responsibility of being a role model seriously and enforces a strict moral code of conduct on his tour bus. He forbids drinking, smoking, and drugs. "Nothing out of order is allowed," he says. "We all need clear heads. Besides, it's important for us to set a good example for our young fans."

Bryan must be doing something right. He has caught the attention of practically everyone in the entertainment field. It seems like everyone has a positive thing to say about him.

Country singer Lisa Brokop says, "I think he's one of the most talented new artists we have today. He deserves every bit of his success."

Singer-songwriter Steve Wariner explains, "He's the most sensitive, kindhearted person I know. I've always said he's the kind of guy you'd like your kids to grow up and be like."

LeAnn Rimes, who teamed with Bryan for the powerful 1998 Something to Talk About tour, says, "He's one of my closest friends. I've known him for four years and he'll be a friend forever."

The critics have also raved about Bryan. *Billboard* wrote: "This guy is the real thing. He's got a voice older than his years, a brilliant song sense and most important he understands what country music is all about. Everyone keeps asking where tomorrow's country stars are—here's one today."

CD Review called Bryan "a perfect balance between innocent youth and emotional maturity." *Cashbox* declared: "White is definitely the heir apparent when it comes to future country superstars."

In 1998 *People* magazine named him one of the Fifty Most Beautiful People in the World. When Bryan was asked how he felt about that honor, he modestly answered, "It feels great, but the first thing I thought when I saw it was, I wish they would have picked a better picture."

E! Entertainment featured Bryan as one of the World's Coolest Bachelors in a segment on the top twenty most eligible celebrity bachelors. Bryan was number eight on the list. His adorable face has also graced the covers of all the major teen and country-music magazines.

How does Bryan feel about all this attention? "It's still not a reality," he says. "I think because I'm so focused on the music, I just don't realize what's actually going on out there. I have been in a major trance.

"A lot of stuff has happened that I wouldn't have expected in a million years," he continues. "The reason it surprises me is that there are so many talented artists out there. How in the world did all this stuff happen to me?"

One surprise was receiving a call from Shania Twain, who wanted Bryan to sing a duet with her for her third album, *Come On Over*. Not surprisingly, the song "From This Moment On" shot to the top of the charts. After meeting him, Shania said, "He probably doesn't realize how cute he really is. He's very sweet and shy."

Part of Bryan's appeal comes from the way he treats his fans. At his concerts, it's not unusual to see thousands of girls clamoring for his autograph. After his performances, Bryan will usually sign autographs for hours. He hates to see anyone go home disappointed.

Bryan is also eager to take part in charity events. After the tragic Oklahoma City bombing in April 1995, Bryan, who grew up near the city, spearheaded a benefit that raised more than $75,000 for scholarships for children injured or orphaned in the blast. He has participated in benefits for the T. J. Martell Foundation, St. Jude

Children's Hospital, the Cystic Fibrosis Foundation, Country CARES, and Boys and Girls Clubs of America, just to name a few.

"I lean toward charities that involve children," he says. "That's where everything starts. It's one of the things that I've wanted to be involved in the most. I love being around kids, and to see kids without the abilities to do the things they want to do, it makes you want to help them achieve their goals. They need people for courage and strength."

Bryan is happy where he is right now. His career is a testimony to hard work, patience, and faith. He's doing the job he really wants to do.

The real Bryan White is caring, considerate, and proud of his wholesome image. "I want to show people who don't dig country that it's not all songs about drinking and cheating on your wife," he says. "It's about real stuff, love and life. I think most of the great lyric-written songs come out of Nashville."

Bryan should know. He not only sings great songs, he writes some of them, too, being one of the most prolific songwriters in country music. Besides writing some of his own material, he cowrote Sawyer Brown's smash hit "I Don't Believe in Goodbye" as well as Diamond Rio's hit "Imagine That."

Bryan is one of the most talented and popular of the new generation of country singers. How he rose from obscurity to the top of the charts is a fascinating story.

Bryan had no thoughts of stardom when he moved to Nashville at the age of eighteen to pursue a career in country music. He just wanted to sing. Today he's playing his music in the big leagues—and he's on a nonstop winning streak!

two

bryan's musical childhood

bryan Shelton White was born on February 17, 1974, in Lawton, Oklahoma, but grew up in Oklahoma City. His parents, Anita and Wilford "Bud" White, Jr., were childhood sweethearts who married young. Anita was just seventeen when Bryan was born; Bud was nineteen.

Bryan inherited his love of music from his parents. Growing up, Bud and Anita dreamed of breaking into the music business. They were both in their early teens when they began singing professionally, trying to make their own mark in music.

Bryan's mom performed with a rhythm and

blues band in rock clubs in and around Oklahoma City, while his dad played classic country music in honky-tonks. In those early years, the young couple had everything in common. They were both striving for a career in music. They also wanted to raise a family. In 1976 Bryan's brother, Daniel, was born. Bud and Anita bought a house in Oklahoma City and raised their boys in a home filled with love and music

"I grew up listening to everything, but it was the country stuff that hit me right here," says Bryan, pointing to his heart.

Bryan is extremely proud of his parents' musical achievements. He says of his mom, "She probably has the best voice of any woman I've ever heard."

The fact that his parents didn't make it big in music didn't discourage them. Bud and Anita never stopped performing. "I have come to the conclusion that the reason that music didn't happen for Mom and Dad is because they had two little boys to raise," explains Bryan. "They thought that was a lot more important, and I'm certainly glad they did."

Bud and Anita instilled the love of music into their boys. Because of this, it is almost as if Bryan was born to entertain. According to Bryan, he's descended from five generations of entertainers.

His great-grandmother was a popular square-dance caller in Oklahoma. His grandfather, Wilford White, a professional auctioneer, gave him early career tips: "You've got to have rhythm, a lot of endurance, and a strong throat."

Bryan knew from the time he was very young that if music was going to be his future, it would be country music. "I've always had that country frame of mind," says Bryan. "I branched out as far as music goes—there isn't any kind of music I don't like—but I grew up in the country, loving country music, and it's what I keep coming back to."

Growing up in Oklahoma, Bryan was surrounded by country music. Along with Bryan, Oklahoma is the home state of such country superstars as Reba McEntire, Garth Brooks, and Vince Gill.

Listening to music set Bryan's young heart pounding. He recalls, "My first five years, I wanted to beat on something all the time." The little drummer boy honed his percussive chops on pots, pans, and cardboard boxes until at age five his parents bought him his first drum set.

From the day he held his first real set of drumsticks, Bryan spent every spare moment practicing what his father taught him. "I think the drums are the backbone of every song," he says. "I really wanted to play the drums."

His childhood years were idealistic, but the contentment Bryan felt didn't last long. While he was still young, his parents divorced amicably. Overnight his world was turned upside down. Luckily, Bryan had the support of his paternal grandparents, Wilford and Shelley White, to help him through the tough times.

"I would say they're a second set of parents," remarks Bryan. "I have two sets of parents. I learned just as much from them as I did from my mom and dad. I wish everybody could meet my grandparents. If a lot of people in the world were like these two people, we wouldn't have any problems. They're two of the most genuine, sweet, kind, and loving people there are."

With the help of his grandparents, Bryan learned to make the best of his situation. Because both his parents remarried, he now had two houses to live in. But the one thing that remained the same was that no matter whom he lived with, there was always music around. Bud and Anita were a consistently strong, positive influence on Bryan and his brother, Daniel. Bryan remains close to his folks and speaks of them frequently in interviews. He credits them with providing an atmosphere that gave him the encouragement to be himself.

As a young boy, Bryan was energetic, impressionable, and shy. A natural talent, he was able to master the drums and later the guitar with incredible ease. But music wasn't the only thing young Bryan loved to do. His two favorite sports were basketball and fishing. While his father and grandfather often took him fishing, it was his grandma Shelley who taught him how to play basketball.

"Bryan just loved basketball," says Shelley. "He never got to play much in high school because the other players were all six feet, five inches tall. If Bryan had played, he could have been a great basketball player. He hit the goal nicely."

Because of his love for the great outdoors, Bryan says his favorite season is summer. But Christmas holds the fondest memories for him. "I think every day ought to be like Christmas—a time to gather with the people you love, celebrate the birth of Christ, and not take things for granted," he says. "It's my favorite holiday because it's the one time out of the whole year when I have nothing booked and I can go home and see my family."

Bryan feels that no matter what age you are, you become a kid again at Christmas time. Because both his parents remarried, Bryan remembers that he celebrated Christmas four or five times every year. "I always remember traveling a lot because we had to cover the four corners of the family," he explains.

Bryan's warmest memories are of celebrating Christmas with his entire family at his grandma Shelley's house. Besides Shelley's famous fudge and punch, Bryan says, there was somebody who got to play Santa Claus every year. "I was always intrigued by it. I was always trying to figure out who it was. I remember that *I* wanted to be Santa Claus," he says.

At age six, Bryan asked his grandma Shelley for a Santa Claus suit. She worked on his costume for a month; she sewed him little red pajamas and made him a beard to go with it. She dressed Daniel like an elf so he could be Bryan's helper.

"We were serving the food and we heard this 'Ho ho ho! Merry Christmas' coming up the hall," remembers Shelley, laughing. "Bryan had filled a pillowcase full of his toys. He'd pull a toy out of the pillowcase, put it on the table, and say, 'Merry Christmas.' Then Daniel would come up behind him and pick up the toy, and Bryan would say, 'You can't keep that—that's mine.' They were adorable."

In addition to wanting to be Santa, Bryan's other holiday tradition was to have "lots of batteries" in the house. His mom recalls that Bryan used to remind her to buy batteries every year. "He used to say, 'Now, Mom, before we go to bed and Santa Claus gets here, we have to have lots of batteries,'" explains Anita. "I'd say, 'Why, Bryan?' He'd say, 'For all the toys, Mom!'"

When he was young, Bryan couldn't wait to open his presents. "When I was a kid, the only thing I thought about was what I was going to get for Christmas," he says. His mother's rule was that he had to wait until Christmas morning to open everything, but he admits his grandma broke that rule. "My grandma spoiled us more than my mom did," says Bryan. "My grandma was the only one who'd let us open a present a day early. My mom would never give in."

One Christmas Eve, Bryan found a way to open his gifts without anyone's seeing him. After everyone went to bed, Bryan and Daniel got up and unwrapped most of their presents. They were really easy to unwrap because his mom didn't use a lot of tape. By the time Anita found everything opened the next morning, Bryan and his brother had already spent most of the night playing with their new toys.

All Bryan's Christmas holidays at home were special, but the one that stands out was when he discovered an early gift at his grandparents' house. "My grandparents had this big house that was built with another section that was meant to be for a maid, but it was always just used for storage," says Bryan. "So I went over there one morning and found a brand-new bike with training wheels on it. I got it out and rode it all around the block without asking. They caught me riding it and sat me down and tried to convince me that it wasn't mine and that Santa Claus was storing it there for some other kid. I believed it and then, lo and behold, on Christmas morning that same bike was there, ready to be ridden again by me."

Today when Bryan goes home to spend time with his family, the material gifts are not that important. According to Bryan, "The greatest gift I've ever received at Christmas time was when everybody woke up, smelled the coffee, and realized what it was all about. It gets better every year."

There were many people in young Bryan's life who shaped him into the fine young man he is today. One very special person in his life was his third-grade teacher, Lou Ann Pogue. She was

Bryan's favorite teacher. He says she treated all students equally. She would go to birthday parties and baseball games. She supported her students in everything they wanted to do. She was one of the first people to encourage Bryan's musical talent.

"She really helped me and changed my life," says Bryan. "She heard me say that on CMT [Country Music Television] and called up my grandma, bawling her head off. She felt that if she could help just one kid, that was her greatest reward. She was a great influence on my life."

Like any other kid interested in music, Bryan juggled schoolwork and drum lessons. When he turned ten, his mom decided to take him to some of her shows. In 1984 Anita opened for Loretta Lynn at a concert in Oklahoma City. It would change Bryan's life forever. "That show pretty much set me on fire," he says. "I was in awe."

By the age of thirteen he was playing drums in many of the Oklahoma City bands formed by his parents. Bryan thought the arrangement was perfect. He loved playing the drums and didn't mind sitting in the back on the stage behind a drum set. He was so shy he felt comfortable in the background. But his stage-savvy mom had other plans for him.

One night she literally forced Bryan to sing. She was at the sound board before one of their gigs when she picked up Bryan's voice coming over the drum microphone. The song was "Stand by Me," and Bryan was still singing when she swung a drum mike in front of his mouth.

"She came over and put the microphone in front of my face," Bryan recalls. "I guess I was nervous, because I kept trying to move my head away from the microphone until my mom told me, 'You better sing, boy.' Finally I got into the mike, and when I finished, she was crying. It was one of the most memorable moments of my life."

Once he got a taste of singing, there was no stopping him. As he approached his high-school years Bryan became more and more serious about singing. When he was in his junior year at Putnam City West High School, he started to play the guitar and began singing and playing in a Christian rock band and a jazz trio. He also began writing his own songs.

Whenever he had a problem with music or lyrics, he went to his mom or dad for advice. Because of their musical knowledge, they were always able to help him. "I think it's really cool to have parents who are musical," says Bryan. "If I play something for my mom, I know she gets it.

Musically, she knows exactly what's going on with my songs. And so does my dad. A lot of kids go through a stage in their life where they don't get along with their parents because they don't want to do what their parents want them to do.

"I went through a stage close to that, but I don't think I was as bad as I could have been because I thought my parents were hip. They always played music. All my friends thought that was the coolest thing. I think it's neat now for my parents to see all of this stuff that's happening to me."

Bryan balanced his education with performing all through his school years. "I tried to mix music and school activities, but in my senior year it interfered," he says. "I didn't go to any football games because I was playing music on weekends. I spent a lot of years in clubs playing with my parents. I considered music part of my life. And I spent time doing it because I wanted to take it to another level."

For a while Bryan considered becoming a lawyer, but now he confesses, "It was just a phase." He always knew he would have a career in country music.

His brother, Daniel, is thrilled that Bryan's getting the chance to do what he loves. "I remember in high school we used to come home and watch TNN [The Nashville Network] after school," says Daniel. "Bryan would tell me, 'I'm going to be on TNN someday.'"

Bryan was deeply inspired by one artist in particular: country singer and songwriter Steve Wariner. When Bryan was fifteen, his grandfather took him to see one of Wariner's concerts. Bryan wrote the singer a two-page letter letting him know what a big fan he was. Then he waited outside Wariner's tour bus and handed it to the first person he saw getting on. After the show, Wariner walked right up to Bryan to shake his hand and thank him for his kind words.

"When Steve played in Oklahoma, I always went to see him," says Bryan. "I met him a couple of times, but I was always just one of the many standing in line. Steve's pretty much been my hero. He's been a huge influence on me as a singer."

In high school, Bryan was singing in clubs every weekend. He was gaining experience and realizing how much he loved performing. Remembering his teenage years, he says, "I was basically the quiet guy. I knew a lot of people, but I wasn't a real social kind of person. Everybody knew I sang and performed, and I think that's the title that most people stuck on my head: 'Oh, that's the guy that sings.' I've never been into the partying scene. It always scared me."

By the time he graduated from Putnam City West High School in 1992, he knew he wanted a career in country music. "I think country music is the most relatable music out there," he says. "I just feel more comfortable singing about morals and things I grew up on." While his friends were busy applying to colleges, Bryan was moving to Music City.

"I had this magnet," he says, "just pulling me to Nashville. It was pretty scary to make the move, but when you are that young, I think you feel invincible to a certain extent. Everybody is full of hopes when they first move to Nashville—and those hopes are so strong that nothing can discourage you.

"When I set my mind to do something and say I'm going to do it, I just have to do it. I knew I wanted to sing; I knew I wanted to play; I knew I wanted to write. I didn't think about anything else. I just packed up and left. My parents were surprised, but I told them, 'I'm not going to let you down.'"

It was especially hard for Wilford White to watch his grandson go. Privately Wilford wanted Bryan to be an auctioneer. "I would have been a fourth-generation auctioneer," explains Bryan.

"I know my grandpa was a little disappointed when I left."

But what was happening in Nashville was just too exciting. A friend of his family introduced Bryan's music to session guitarist Billy Joe Walker, Jr., who was looking for an act to produce. Another mutual friend sent Bryan's tapes off to Glen Campbell Music.

In the summer of 1992 Bryan made two trips to Nashville. He met a few people, including Billy Joe Walker, Jr. Walker liked Bryan's sound, but he was honest with the aspiring singer. "If you want to have a career in Nashville, you have to live here," Walker told Bryan. "When you plan on moving to Nashville, come back and see me." Bryan felt that a window of opportunity was opening for him, and he wasn't sure it would open again. He didn't want to pass it up, so he made the decision to leave Oklahoma.

By this time, his family saw how serious and ambitious he was about the music business. "Nobody ever discouraged me," he recalls. "My family said, 'Okay, if that's what you want, here's five hundred dollars. Now go after it.'" Bryan's grandfather even gave Bryan his road-weary Plymouth Horizon for his trip to Nashville.

At the age of eighteen, Bryan said goodbye to his family in Oklahoma and set out to see if he could break into country music. Armed with an abundance of determination, talent, and optimism, he had a clear goal: to get a record deal.

All he had with him was his guitar, a few songs he had written, and a dream. In less than one year he would find out he was exactly what Nashville executives were looking for.

three

next stop, nashville

When Bryan arrived in Nashville on October 1, 1992, country music was enjoying an enormous rise in popularity, thanks in part to the success of artists Garth Brooks, Reba McEntire, Alan Jackson, and Vince Gill. A long-overdue youth movement was in full swing. New labels were emerging, and they were more anxious to sign up new artists than at any other time in country-music history.

Bryan was in the right place at the right time. Two days after he arrived in Music City, he took Billy Joe Walker, Jr., up on his previous offer and went to see him again. He was hoping to get some advice from Walker and maybe a recommendation. The renowned guitarist was well known in Nashville. If Walker called a manager, record company executive, or music publisher, they usually listened. Bryan was hoping Walker would give him the encouragement he needed.

He did. Walker was so overwhelmed by Bryan's talent, he told him he wanted to work with him. According to Bryan, Walker believed in him from day one.

During his first three months in Music City, things moved fast for Bryan. In January 1993 he met with Marty Gamblin from Glen Campbell Music and GC Management.

The two companies were owned by singer Glen Campbell, who was a big star in the 1960s and 1970s. Campbell had put Marty Gamblin in charge of finding new stars because he had a good track record for spotting talent. In the early 1990s he discovered country superstar Alan Jackson and gave him his first big break. When Gamblin met Bryan, he saw in the young man from Oklahoma the same qualities he'd seen in Jackson and was immediately won over by Bryan's high-energy performance and charisma. He signed Bryan to a management contract and started to shop his tape around the record labels.

Bryan was off to a good start, but he had to have patience. Even though things started falling into place for him, success didn't happen overnight. Billy Joe Walker and Marty Gamblin knocked on a lot of doors and had numerous rejections. There was no record deal yet.

In the meantime, Bryan was running low on cash. He recalls, "For the first year I had to have my family wire me money every month."

One of the ways budding singers get known in Nashville is by singing demos of other people's songs. Bryan thought it was a good way to get noticed and to make a little extra money. First he started off singing demos of a couple of songs he'd written. Then other people began hearing of him.

"I was in a recording studio singing some demos, and a couple of musicians were there and they said to me, 'Would you sing one of *our* songs?'" says Bryan. From there things snowballed. More and more songwriters and musicians liked Bryan's smooth sound and requested his time. He was soon one of the busiest demo singers on Nashville's Music Row, getting paid forty dollars a pop to sing other people's songs.

Some of the songs Bryan demoed became hits by *other* people. But that didn't discourage him.

He knew it was the nature of the business. Besides, most country singers got their start singing demos. Garth Brooks, Trisha Yearwood, and Joe Diffie were all demo singers before hitting it big.

Bryan also worked as a busboy at High Noon Saloon on the outskirts of Nashville. Some nights he'd bring his guitar to the club and perform for the sparse crowd. He kept telling himself that it was all a great learning experience and that in the end it would work out.

But there were times he doubted if he'd ever succeed in country music. There were so many young singers pouring into Nashville every day. Most of them found themselves on a bus going back home before ever being given a chance to prove they were good. Bryan didn't want that to happen to him. He was going to stay in town, no matter how long it took.

Billy Joe Walker tried generating interest in Bryan at Asylum Records, which was starting a Nashville division. But Kyle Lehning, the label's president, passed on Bryan. It seemed as if everywhere Walker and Gamblin went with Bryan, they heard the same thing: "He's too young, he doesn't have enough experience." So Marty Gamblin set out to change that.

Gamblin played a big part in shaping Bryan's career. He introduced Bryan to a country band he was managing called Pearl River. The band, which had minor success in the early 1990s, was going on tour, and Gamblin thought it would be a good idea if Bryan went along.

Bryan's job was selling souvenirs for the band, but it was perhaps the best job he ever took. On the road he became friends with Derek George, Pearl River's guitarist. Derek was a hot young talent who'd been raised on rock but had an amazing feel for country and blues. Bryan and Derek had a lot in common.

"Derek and I were both eighteen when we met," says Bryan. "We were hanging around these forty-year-olds, so we were the two youngest people around. He knows me better than anybody. We are just alike. I totally consider us brothers."

It wasn't long before they started writing songs together. There was no certainty that any of their songs would ever be recorded. But that didn't stop Bryan and Derek from churning out what they hoped would become hits.

It's difficult to understand the kind of dedication that motivates an artist like Bryan White. When he started writing songs with Derek, neither of them had much success. Still, everything they wrote was fresh and fun.

They wrote their tunes on the band's bus as it traveled from town to town. Once they got to a venue where Pearl River would be playing, they continued to write between sound checks and even sometimes after the concerts. During Pearl River's shows, Bryan worked as a vendor selling T-shirts and posters to their fans.

One night Derek asked the band if Bryan could join them onstage for a song. The guys in Pearl River saw how serious Bryan was about pursuing a singing career. They started to let him sing one song at every show. Bryan remembers, "I'd be in the booth selling T-shirts and hats and I would hear Derek saying, 'We have a new guy we want you to meet—Bryan White.' I would get someone to take my place in the booth and run to the stage and perform one song."

Brinson Strickland, another member of Pearl River, says, "Bryan was always a better singer than a T-shirt salesman."

Bryan says of his early experience on the road, "I thought it was great to go out on tour with Pearl River. I got a chance to see what it felt like being on the road and seeing how everything worked. Plus they let me sing one of my songs onstage every night." Now all Bryan was hoping for was his own shot at success.

His luck soon changed. Asylum Records president Kyle Lehning agreed to meet Bryan again.

Billy Joe Walker didn't see any reason why Asylum shouldn't take a chance on Bryan. The label needed a hot young artist to get them off the ground. Walker thought Bryan was the perfect candidate.

But it took some convincing. Even though Lehning was initially impressed with Bryan, he didn't jump at the chance to add him to the Asylum roster. "He said he just really wanted to see me bloom a little more," says Bryan. "I was eighteen at the time, so that was something that was definitely a factor to him. He wanted to figure out what I wanted to do for direction and find out a little bit more about me before signing me. I'm glad that he did that rather than throw me into the pile of artists."

Lehning, who'd had success producing Randy Travis, knew real talent when he heard it. "When Bryan came into my office with his guitar and started singing, I was blown away," he says. "I found him to be eminently talented and great-looking. He had an obvious natural talent. But I wasn't sure about signing him. You have to understand that no label had yet signed an artist as young as Bryan was. He finally convinced me to take a chance on him."

Bryan signed his deal with Asylum in 1993.

One year after arriving in Nashville, he got the break he'd been dreaming about. His debut album was scheduled to be released the following year.

Billy Joe Walker, Jr., and Kyle Lehning were the album's producers. They had the job of overseeing the recording sessions. They hired the musicians, helped Bryan choose the songs, and made decisions on the final mixing of the tracks. Nashville has known some great producers in its rich history, and Kyle Lehning ranks as one of the best working today. Bryan considered himself lucky to have Lehning and Walker produce his debut album.

The first order of business was finding the right songs for Bryan's album. Choosing songs is the most crucial factor for a new artist, and Bryan was very selective about what went on his first disc.

He was given almost total artistic freedom, but his producers really helped him put everything together. He felt lucky to surround himself with enthusiastic professionals who shared his vision.

"We all kind of talked about what we wanted to do," says Bryan. "Kyle and Billy took what I'm about and enhanced it. All through the recording, they had a lot of neat ideas. We collaborated on almost everything. If they had an idea, they ran it by me, or if I had an idea, I ran it by them. Kyle and Billy are really passionate about making music, and we've become good friends."

Over the next few months, Bryan began cutting songs for his first album. He recorded the tracks at Nashville's Nightingale Studio and The Sound Emporium. The overdubs were done at Imagine Sound Studio, and the album was mixed at Morningstar Sound Studio.

Bryan was so excited to be in the studio recording his first album. "It was like one big party," he says. "Billy played guitar on some tracks. Kyle played piano. I asked Derek to sing background vocals. The whole process of being in the studio and putting something on tape that will be released to the public is so satisfying. It's such an adrenaline rush."

Bryan felt fortunate to be working alongside so many experienced and talented people. In his quest for the best tunes, he recorded songs written by some of Nashville's top writers, like Skip Ewing, Bob DiPiero, and Jim Weatherly.

Some songs chosen for Bryan's debut release were sentimental ballads, like "Someone Else's Star" and "Rebecca Lynn." Others had snappy rock and pop influences, like "Eugene You Genius" and "This Town." Bryan cowrote two songs, the melodic "You Know How I Feel" and the catchy "Look at Me Now."

He wanted his music to be meaningful. "I like to sing about things I like to hear about," says Bryan. "Songs about family. You know, like a little kid trying on his dad's shoes for the first time and hoping he'll grow into them one day. Those are the songs I like. And that's what I wanted on my first album."

With his debut single and album scheduled to be released in the fall of 1994, Bryan White was finally on his way.

four

new kid in country

the only song Bryan wasn't completely thrilled with on his self-titled debut album was the song "Eugene You Genius." So you can imagine how surprised he was when the record company decided to release it as the first single.

"Eugene You Genius," which Bryan describes as "a straight-ahead rocking tune with quirky lyrics," was released to radio on September 19, 1994. Hopes were high, especially since Bryan was being touted as one of the hottest new artists in town.

One month earlier he had debuted the song at the Warner/Elektra/Atlantic New Faces show, held at Nashville's legendary, newly renovated Ryman Auditorium. Bryan and a half dozen young artists performed songs from their upcoming albums. But it was Bryan who set the Ryman rocking.

The five hundred invited guests included radio disc jockeys and record buyers. After seeing Bryan in action, disc jockeys from country stations all across the United States were interested in talking to him.

"I couldn't believe I was playing in such a famous building," Bryan told one deejay. "I mean, the Ryman is the former home of the Grand Ole Opry. There is such history that went on in there. Hank Williams, Sr., played on that stage. And now I was playing there."

Every disc jockey who met Bryan was taken with him. He was such a refreshingly down-to-earth guy, you couldn't help liking him. He was going to have no trouble getting his songs played on the radio. He just wasn't aware that he'd have to go on a promotional tour and personally introduce himself to each and every country-music disc jockey.

"That was a big adjustment for me," he says. "I had my own views of what I thought it was going to be like before I moved to Nashville. I thought it was going to be nothing but singing. It turned out being so much more.

"About thirty percent of being an artist is being a singer," he adds. "The rest is promotions and interviews. Once I started doing more press, that's when I started realizing, 'This is something I'm going to have to get used to.' As a kid I didn't realize that that was such a big part of it."

In the beginning, Bryan was completely inexperienced in handling himself with reporters and disc jockeys. "When I first started going out on the radio tour, I was a little bit overdramatic," he explains. "I learned not to be intimidated by anyone. I also had to learn to become comfortable and confident."

Bryan went on a five-month radio promotional tour to promote his single and debut album. Sometimes he'd travel to three cities in one day. He'd walk into a radio station, either at six in the morning or six at night, and he'd sing in a conference room for whoever was at the station. Bryan remembers, "I'd sing four or five tunes for them. I'd say things like, 'Hey, I'm Bryan White and I've got an album coming out. I hope you play my record.' "

Country-music stations were eager to play a new song from a fresh, new talent. All across the United States, stations blasted Bryan's single "Eugene You Genius" over the airwaves. But the song bombed. While some critics thought it was "a fun barroom romp," others disregarded it as a "silly single that might do more harm than good to new artist Bryan White."

Bryan's instincts about "Eugene You Genius" may have been right. "The single didn't do anything," he explains. "It went to number forty on the charts and died. It was a song I wasn't completely nuts about. But at the time, everyone thought it was the safest one to release."

Even though the single was not a huge hit, it introduced Bryan to country-music radio audiences. When his debut album, *Bryan White,* hit stores on October 11, 1994, it was a day of celebration for Bryan. He was anxious to talk about it.

In one interview he described his album as "a big mix of everything. It's a conglomerate. There's a lot of country traditional stuff, there are some things that are R&B. It's kind of a soulful type of album—something different compared to what's out there now."

Bryan couldn't believe he was actually holding his first CD in his hands. The cover photo pictures twenty-year-old Bryan gazing dreamily into the camera. He looks gorgeous; he's dressed all in black and has on a cropped jacket. His hair is longer than he wears it now.

Inside there are two photos of Bryan as a baby and one photo of him at age ten playing the drums. In the liner notes he graciously thanks everyone who ever believed in his talent and who helped him get started. He even gives a special mention to "Steve Wariner for being such a positive influence in my career and for your friendship."

He dedicated his album "to my mom and dad. Thanks for all of your love, encouragement, and for passing along to me your gift of music. If I do indeed possess the talent and skills to be a successful recording artist and performer, I owe it all to you. See what you created. I love you."

Critics gave Bryan's debut effort rave reviews. "A nice Nashville surprise," wrote one critic. "White sounds comfortable and convincing on sentimental tunes like 'Rebecca Lynn' and 'Someone Else's Star,' and has fun with the album's moderately successful first single, 'Eugene You Genius.'"

Of course, Bryan was hoping to become a major contender in country music. But at just twenty years old, he knew it would take some time. Crowded charts are a constant struggle for the new kids in country. And Bryan was no exception.

"There are so many big artists that there's this wall we have to try and break through," he says. "It's hard for us little guys to get through it. Every once in a while a new artist is able to do it. But it's tough."

Bryan wasn't an overnight sensation, but he was slowly rising on the country-music charts. His album was selling well, and in March 1995 his second single, "Look at Me Now," was released. "Look at Me Now" is a very special song to Bryan. He cowrote it with Derek George and John Tirro, and it remains his favorite.

"It was my first top-twenty record," Bryan says proudly. "That slowly started introducing me to everybody out there."

Things really took off for Bryan when his third and fourth singles, "Someone Else's Star" and "Rebecca Lynn," were released. Both songs zoomed up the charts to the number-one position.

"I think at that point—between those two songs—is where the train took off and I was barely hanging on," says Bryan, smiling. "It was like, 'Hey, it's time to go. Things are starting to move.' At that point, my career started to kick in at a faster pace."

Kenny Hamlin, senior vice president at Asylum Records, says, "There was no question that we believed Bryan was a star from the beginning. We were going to keep our noses to the grindstone until it happened. And no matter what the request was, no one at the label ever questioned why we were staying with Bryan and his record. They just said yes to everything."

According to Bryan, the fact that he was one of the first artists signed to Asylum's country label was a plus. He felt lucky that Asylum gave him so much attention and support.

"Every time I play somewhere, there's somebody there representing me from my label," says Bryan. "It makes me happy to know that they're really supportive and they want to be there to represent me well."

When his third and fourth singles vaulted into the number-one spot, he thought more about Asylum than himself. "Because I was signed to a brand-new label, I was glad to be the first person to do that for them," he said in one interview.

In 1995 Bryan went out on the road to promote his album. Because he was a new artist, he opened shows for bigger names like Pam Tillis, Diamond Rio, George Jones, Randy Travis, and Tracey Lawrence. It was a great training ground for Bryan. Opening for better-established artists gave Bryan the opportunity to introduce himself to audiences and gain some recognition.

For these concerts, Bryan had no band. The powerhouse concerts with throbbing amplifiers would come later. For now, Bryan sat alone on a stage with his acoustic guitar and sang his songs.

A lot of young acts begin by playing these acoustic shows. But Bryan wasn't used to it. "It was tough," he says. "I look back on it now and think the experience made me a much better player and singer. But there was no one to hide behind and no one to catch me if something went wrong."

He was thrilled when Marty Gamblin told him it was time to put together a band. Gamblin suggested hiring members of Pearl River. By that time the band had lost its recording contract with Capitol Records and was in need of a job. Bryan thought it was a perfect idea, especially since he was such good friends with Derek George. Bryan's band would include Derek on lead guitar and vocals, Brinson Strickland on guitar and vocals, Joe Morgan on bass, Monty Booker on drums, Joe Rogers on steel guitar, fiddle, and squeeze box, and Tom Bently on keyboards.

Bryan couldn't have hoped for a better group of guys. The pairing of Bryan and the band brought his live shows to a whole new level. Not only did the band give him solid backing on-stage, but they also became some of his best friends.

Around the middle of 1995 Asylum told Bryan to get started on a follow-up album. Even though there was still life left in his debut CD, Asylum wanted his sophomore album out by the spring of 1996. Bryan found himself working at break-neck pace, writing songs, recording, and continuing to tour.

"Time was real scarce," he recalls. "I didn't have a whole lot of time to sit down and think about what I was doing or the overall gist of the album. Every time I'd get a chance, I'd swing in, go to the studio, work on it a little bit, and then go back out on the road."

Bryan closed out 1995 on a high note. In November he fulfilled his dream of playing his music at the world-famous Grand Ole Opry in Nashville. He was scheduled to appear on Saturday, November 25.

Backstage before the show, Bryan was both excited and nervous. When he walked into his dressing room, he was surprised to see Steve Wariner. "I walked in and couldn't believe he was there," says Bryan. "We were sharing the same dressing room. We sat around and picked and sang a little bit. It was incredible."

Bryan talked to Pam Tillis and fellow Oklahoman Vince Gill, who were also in the show. And he tried to calm down. But that was easier said than done.

Everyone backstage wished Bryan luck as he got ready for his performance. He could hear singer Ricky Skaggs begin to introduce him. "Ladies and gentlemen, we have with us tonight a brand-new artist I think you're really going to enjoy," announced Skaggs. "Please welcome Bryan White!"

Bryan panicked. His mouth turned to cotton. The audience applauded wildly, but Bryan couldn't move. "Does anybody have something to drink?" he pleaded. "Anything!"

Someone handed him a drink, and he ran out onstage. The first few notes of "Someone Else's Star" began, and Bryan began to sing his number-one song. As excited fans rushed to the front of the stage to take pictures of Bryan, he caught a glimpse of his grandma weeping softly in the front row. She had traveled from Oklahoma to see Bryan perform. Remembering that night, he says, "Grandma had a great time. When it was over, I took her around and gave her the whole Nashville tour."

The rousing welcome Bryan received from the audience was a bit overwhelming for him, but his performance brought the house down. "By the first chorus, the whole crowd was applauding," remembers Bryan. "I couldn't believe it. I almost broke down and couldn't sing. It was hard to hold the tears back."

As 1995 came to a close, Bryan looked back on a terrific year. His debut release was certified gold in December, selling 500,000 copies. (It has since been certified platinum, with more than one million copies sold.)

In an interview Bryan said, "The whole year was like one great big Christmas present. I am so lucky. Right now I'm laying the foundation for what I want to do for the rest of my life. Things are going the best they possibly can and I'm so thankful for it."

five

between now
and forever

the January 31, 1996, issue of *USA Today* blared the headline "Bryan White Lights Teenage Hearts Afire." The article went on to say, "Nashville's newest and youngest—and perhaps cutest—star has recently been tailed by teen magazines."

Bryan was hot, but he was about to get hotter. Teenage girls discovered him, and they loved him. At first Bryan wasn't aware that he was becoming a teen heartthrob. It was something that happened slowly. When his songs "Someone Else's Star" and "Rebecca Lynn" both went to number one, he noticed his audiences were getting younger and younger.

"One of the first times I remember girls screaming, I think, was in an airport," he says. "Some girls were waiting for me to get off the plane. It really caught me off guard. I asked them, 'Are you waiting for me, or is there somebody else back there?' They said, 'We're waiting for you. We want your autograph!' I thought, 'This is pretty cool. Something's happening here.'"

As Bryan gained popularity more teenagers started coming to his shows. But there was a problem. At the time, Bryan was appearing at country music clubs where the audience is required to buy alcohol. Teenagers were not allowed inside them.

When it was announced that Bryan would be coming to one of these clubs, Bryan's fans flocked to see him. But when they arrived, they were shut out because they were underage. Some of them would wait outside in the parking lot and listen to his show.

Bryan didn't know this was going on. One chilly night, after he finished his show at a San Diego club called In Cahoots, he found a group of shivering youngsters waiting outside for him. Ranging in age from five to eighteen, they were excited to meet Bryan and asked for his autograph. As he started signing he asked why they were out in the cold.

Bryan remembers, "They said, 'Well, we couldn't get in, but we could hear from the parking lot and you sounded great.' I figured it was just that one club, but then it started happening everywhere I played. A lot of kids couldn't get into the clubs I was playing at because there was an age limit. A lot of little girls would come with their moms and wait outside the doors. Some of them would travel for two hours to come and see me. It meant something to them and it meant something to me."

Bryan had an idea. He says, "We thought, 'Why not start letting the young fans in the clubs during the sound check hours?' We started doing what we called 'teen shows.' That way our young fans could see our show and hang out with us in the afternoon at the same clubs their parents would visit at night." The all-age shows Bryan did became extremely popular.

Bryan was thrilled with his fast-growing popularity with kids. When his face started popping up in teen magazines, he told one reporter, "I never thought I'd be in a teen magazine. It's exciting to flip through the pages and see your picture. That's a big honor."

When he was asked about the poster-sized pinups of himself in the magazines, he grinned and replied, "If my poster from a teen magazine ends up on the walls of thousands of teenage girls, I think that's pretty cool."

In the early months of 1996, Bryan's popularity continued to soar. So many young fans were showing up at his shows, it was becoming national news. At the honky-tonk Cowboys in Dallas, Texas, something unexpected happened. Bryan played the club's Young Guns show and caused a sensation.

In 1991 Cowboys started booking the hottest new stars in country music for a series of shows they called Young Guns. Over the years, every new artist to come onto the country scene has taken part in these shows. They were all successful. But when Bryan played at Cowboys, more than two thousand fans eagerly lined up to see him. When he took the stage, the roar from the crowd was deafening.

"Bryan took twenty-two hundred kids by storm," says Cowboys representative Dawn Weeks. "Not since we started this series in 1991 with Brooks and Dunn has the noise been so high. Bryan's scream factor was on Elvis level."

Seventy percent of the audience were teenage girls. There was no alcohol served. The only adults present were parents and guardians. Everyone got the chance to see Bryan's hot-as-a-pistol show. As the girls shrieked and sighed for Bryan, he smiled and thanked everyone for coming.

Bryan has been called the bridge that brought young fans to country music. And he's happy with the title. "When I was in school, everyone hated country music," he says. "They were embarrassed to say they listened to it. I'm glad I was able to help pull in young fans. There are a lot of artists my age that are coming out, and kids are paying attention."

The news that teens were screaming for Bryan sent Nashville's Music Row reeling. The majority of country artists at that time were thirty or older. Bryan was the first young artist signed to a major label. He was the first to become a teen idol and lure in teenage listeners. But he wouldn't be the last.

Because of his success in the teen market, other labels started searching for artists in their twenties or younger who could be just as appealing as Bryan. More young singers were signed to Nashville labels than ever before. Artists like David Kersh, Rhett Akins, Kenny Chesney, and Chely Wright were all scoring hits on the charts. Curb Records followed this trend by signing twelve-year-old LeAnn Rimes. LeAnn's first album, *Blue,* debuted at number one on the *Billboard* country album chart and number three on the *Billboard 200* pop album chart. With three more big-selling albums to her credit so far, LeAnn has become country's teen queen.

Bryan remains country's young king. He's flattered by all the attention he receives from his fans. "I'm doing what I do for them," he says. Bryan feels he has captured the hearts of young listeners with songs they can relate to. "I think the reason we have attracted a lot of the younger fans is that they see our energy and dedication," he notes. "Sometimes kids have to have something to relate to. If kids see somebody close to their own age doing something, they are drawn to it. I think that's been the key with the popularity of country music with kids. They can see we've put our minds into it and that we really love what we are doing. That gives them hope to do what they really want, no matter what it is."

While Bryan has the qualities that appeal to young girls, his music is good enough to appeal to adults, too. A publicist at Asylum Records said in an interview, "Bryan backs up his teen heart-throb appeal with his talent and great songs. One of the teen publications said that he was 'totally crushworthy.' I'm sure some of those girls feel that way, but I don't think you could have number-one records based on being 'totally crushworthy.' He has fans that range in age from four to eighty. They all love him."

That was definitely true. By the time Bryan's second album, *Between Now and Forever,* was released in March 1996, he was a full-fledged star with fans of all ages. *Between Now and Forever* debuted at number seven on *Billboard*'s country album chart. After the success of his debut release, many wondered what Bryan would do for an encore.

He was ready to show them. In his career-launching first year, he performed more than two hundred concerts and traveled throughout Canada and the United States. He heard his voice on radio stations everywhere. Girls began to scream for him. Somewhere during his travels, he grew up.

"I was forced to grow up because of all the responsibility," he says. For *Between Now and Forever,* Bryan worked with producers Billy Joe Walker and Kyle Lehning on finding songs that were more emotional and serious. He was dedicated to creating an album that sounded different from his first release. And he succeeded. In a little over one year, Bryan White went from boy wonder to maturing star.

He cowrote four songs on his second album. "My knowledge of writing songs started to really mature on *Between Now and Forever*," he says. "The songs were more believable and energetic. When I look back on my first two albums, I can't believe how different they are. The ideas flew out of me a lot quicker the second time around."

Bryan feels that he found his niche as an artist with *Between Now and Forever*. "This album is definitely more about me," he said at the time of its release. "It's more mature and full of great songs. I know exactly what works for me now." Even though the album was a lot of fun for him to make, he was under a lot more pressure. Because time was in short supply, Bryan found that he had to learn to pace himself. The result was a CD he was extremely proud of.

Between Now and Forever begins on a high note with the scampering country rocker "Sittin' on Go." The song was written by Josh Leo and Rick Bowles. Bryan remembers that Billy Joe Walker first played the song for him. "Around the second verse, I was laughing because I liked it so much," says Bryan. "I laugh when something sounds good to me. It's just my thing. It must be

Billy's, too, because I looked at him and he was cracking up."

Slowing the pace, the album's next track is Mac McAnally's mournful "Still Life," which is a sad song about pain and loss. When Bryan first moved to Nashville, he first became aware of McAnally's powerful songs. " 'Still Life' was one of the first songs my friends and I would play all the time," he says. "It's a song that a lot of people have lived. I think everybody loses somebody, and this song speaks to those who have lost someone."

Bryan cowrote "Blindhearted" with Randy Goodrum, who has written a lot of great songs, including Anne Murray's "You Needed Me." Bryan was honored to write with Goodrum and delighted with their composition. "It's a really cool song," says Bryan. "It fits the vibe of the record. It's unlike anything else I've ever heard."

The irresistibly catchy "Nickel in the Well" was penned by Lonnie Wilson and Chris Waters. It is about a guy saying he'll do anything in the world to get the girl of his dreams.

Bryan's tenor voice reaches an emotional peak in the brokenhearted "I'm Not Supposed to Love You Anymore." The song is a bittersweet ode to love gone wrong. It was written by Skip

Ewing and Donny Kees, who were responsible for Bryan's two smash hits "Someone Else's Star" and "Rebecca Lynn." Bryan explains, "I don't know how Skip Ewing writes such great songs so consistently. This is one of the strongest songs I've ever heard. Bonnie Raitt had it on hold for a long time. The day she let go of it, we snatched it up. At first I was worried, like, 'Do you think I can sing this?' To tell you the truth, I could barely get through it in the studio, because the story line was killing me the whole time."

Bryan and his collaborators Derek George and John Tirro, who wrote "Look at Me Now," teamed again for the guitar-driven country-pop stomper "So Much for Pretending." The tune has an interesting history behind it. "We wrote it right after sound check at a show," says Bryan. "Everyone else in the band had gone back to the hotel and was going to eat and get cleaned up. But Derek and I stayed on the bus. We started plunking out this riff and got a little part of the song going. When we got home, we showed it to John. We all wrote 'Look at Me Now' together, and we felt the same electricity when we wrote this song. The night we finished it was Halloween, and I was going out to visit haunted houses with my dad. We were singing it all night.

We demoed it two or three days later. I played drums, Derek played all the guitars. Derek and I sang all the harmonies, and John played the keyboards. My producers liked the demo so much that they wanted to copy everything on there, which is pretty much what they did. The vocals you hear are the ones we recorded at my house."

Bryan wrote the album's title track, "Between Now and Forever," with George Teren and Don Pfrimmer. Bryan was driving into town one morning to write with the two composers and thought up the title on the way. He had written some of the melody in 1993 but didn't have any lyrics or ideas for it. When he got to the songwriters' office, the trio started writing other tunes. But nothing was working. Bryan remembers he had a strange feeling. He debated whether or not he should tell George and Don about his song. "I finally said, 'I've got this idea, and I have a melody that may go with it—or may not—but it's called "Between Now and Forever."' We started writing and finished it that day. The song asks, 'What are you doing between now and forever?' like it's just an everyday conversational thing. When I thought of it, I thought, 'Wow, that's what I'm going to say to the girl I ask to marry one day.'"

The album next slides into the sunny optimism of "A Hundred and One." Bryan only had to listen to this song once to know that it worked for him. Written by Rich Wayland, Mary Ann Kennedy, and Kye Fleming, it is a great story about two people falling in love and making it last forever. "It makes me think of my grandparents, because they've been together for almost fifty years," says Bryan. "That's the kind of love that doesn't exist too much these days. And it makes you kind of wish that would come back around—that old-fashioned quality of love. That's why I enjoy singing it so much."

Bryan cowrote the ballad "On Any Given Night" with Allison Mellon and Jeff Ross. Bryan says the song was a real turning point for him as a writer. "I'm real proud of it," he states. "I cowrote it with two of my best friends, and neither of them had ever had a song cut before. If you've got somebody out there who is giving you all they've got, then you need to pay attention to that and don't ever lose sight of it, or you could end up empty-handed."

The album ends with the heart-wrenching "That's Another Song," which was written by John Paul Daniel, Monty Powell, Doug Pincock, and Jule Medders. It was one of the first songs Bryan heard for the album, and he didn't have to play it a second time. "I knew from the first moment that I wanted this on the album," he recalls. "I can't say enough about it. I think it's a great traditional country song."

Cut by cut, Bryan's second album was a surefire hit. Critics unanimously praised it. *The Tennessean* called *Between Now and Forever* "serious fun. Bryan White turns in a likeable and emotional CD." *The Dallas Morning News* wrote: "Bryan White needn't worry about sophomore jinx. He proves he's more than a one-album wonder. His supple singing style—a clear voice that conveys innocence and honesty—sounds more confident now." *Billboard* said: "White has silenced his skeptics. He's not just emoting emotions; he's feeling them. Here, he shows that he handles boogie as well as ballads. It doesn't hurt that he's also a good writer."

The first single off *Between Now and Forever* was "I'm Not Supposed to Love You Anymore," which was released in June 1996. It burned up the charts to the number-one spot. It was Bryan's third consecutive number-one single, and also his third consecutive ballad.

Was Bryan nervous about being typecast as a balladeer? "I can't say it didn't cross my mind," he offers. "I do not want to be noticed as just a balladeer. I want people to feel like that is something I do well, but my show is jam-packed with rocking energy. We throw people a lot with the live show."

Everyone involved with Bryan's career wondered how country radio would react to an up-tempo number. They would soon find out. The succession of Bryan's hits was masterfully programmed by the crafty folks at Asylum Records. While one song was riding high on the charts, they were planning the release of another. After the success of "I'm Not Supposed to Love You Anymore," Asylum next released "So Much for Pretending," which also zoomed into the number-one position. The third single out was "That's Another Song," which eased up the charts and settled into the top ten. The last single released off *Between Now and Forever* was "Sittin' on Go," which flew up to number one in just a few weeks. In record time, Bryan had five number-one hits out of eight singles released.

The expectations for Bryan kept getting higher with each success. But he says he didn't feel any pressure. "I haven't felt pressure since my singles have done so well," he says. "It's the people around me who feel more pressure than I do. When I recorded the second album, I just said, 'Chill. All you can do is the best you can do.' If you get too caught up in the whole thing, you get away from why you're in this in the first place."

With two hot-selling albums cemented on the charts, Bryan had achieved more than anyone had thought possible. But in many ways he was still in the beginning stages of his red-hot career. For Bryan White, the best was yet to come.

six

the right place

With his first two albums certified hits, Bryan had accomplished half of what it takes to be a major success in the music business. The other half included touring, giving interviews, and shooting music videos of his hit songs. The latter was the most important.

Music videos are sometimes the reason why a new singer becomes a star. The videos of Bryan's first four singles ("Eugene You Genius," "Look at Me Now," "Rebecca Lynn," and "Someone Else's Star") became big hits and permanent fixtures on Country Music Television (CMT) and The Nashville Network (TNN).

CMT supported Bryan's career right from the beginning. "He is one of the fastest-rising artists we've seen in a long time," says Tracey Rogers, director of programming at CMT. "Bryan is a very talented singer, songwriter, and musician who is meticulous about the quality of his music and videos. CMT viewers continually let us know about how much they love Bryan."

The videos of his songs are like minimovies. Each one tells the story of the song. Bryan explains, "I think it is interesting for fans to see the translation of songs to video form. I have always believed that music videos are very important in establishing the fans' visual awareness of an artist and helping fans connect the artist to their music."

It wasn't long before Bryan became a video star. CMT selected him as the Rising Male Video Star of 1995 and the Male Video Artist of 1996. CMT also named Bryan their monthly Showcase Artist for October 1996. Not only did they put together a half-hour profile on Bryan, but they continually ran all seven of his music videos throughout the month. As if all that wasn't enough, Bryan was honored when "Rebecca Lynn" and "I'm Not Supposed to Love You Anymore" captured two of the top ten spots on the CMT 1996 Video Countdown.

Bryan's two clips were singled out for dramatic storytelling and a powerhouse performance. Of all Bryan's videos, "Rebecca Lynn" remains his favorite. It tells the story of childhood friends who eventually marry. As the sun-drenched video unfolds, fresh-faced Bryan captures poignancy and charm. He found the filming of "Rebecca Lynn" to be calm and enjoyable.

But the video shoot of "Someone Else's Star" was the complete opposite. To this day, Bryan says it was the most hectic video he ever worked on. "We started filming it at ten in the morning and the shoot lasted until two the next morning," he says. "I was a little uncomfortable, because some of my friends came to the set and were watching me. That freaked me out. Then I lost my voice from singing. There was this cloud of hair spray around me all the time. And they kept applying makeup to my face.

"John Lloyd Miller was the director, and he was a blast to work with. He just told me, 'We've got a job to do. Let's hang out and have fun and do it.' "

With his videos, Bryan stretched his talents beyond singing and into the acting arena. "The more you do them, the easier they get," he says. "I've found the process of shooting videos more fun with every one we did."

At this point in his career Bryan could have slowed down. But he was ready to do more. Instead of sitting back and enjoying his success, he sped up the pace, even though it was sometimes exhausting. Bryan told a reporter, "As long as I'm doing something musical, I'm always happy. I like to work. There's no time to get bored."

All his hard work was paying off. Bryan began to be recognized by the industry as the most talented new artist in country music. Soon the accolades came pouring in. He was crowned Top New Male Vocalist at the Academy of Country Music Awards. He won Best New Artist and Single of the Year (for "Rebecca Lynn") at the Entertainment Radio Networks Country Radio Music Awards, and SRO named him New Touring Artist of the Year.

He was honored to win the Male Star of Tomorrow trophy at the TNN/Music City News Country Awards. The award meant a lot to Bryan because it came from the fans. The annual event allows fans to vote for their favorites through ballots in *Music City News* magazine and special phone numbers. The awards show was held at the Grand Ole Opry on June 10, 1996, and telecast live on TNN.

As Bryan walked to the stage to accept his award, the fans in the balcony were cheering his name. Dressed in a tan suit, he looked great, and he was smiling from ear to ear as he gave his acceptance speech. Clutching the award, he said, "Thank you so much. This has been a really great year for me." Then, before he left the stage, he pointed to his fans in the balcony and said, "This one goes to all of you. I love you."

Backstage in the press room, Bryan answered every question the reporters asked him. They wanted to know about his songwriting, his concerts, his albums, how he felt about his teen idol status, and what was ahead for him. "The teen idol thing is fun," he said, smiling. "We're on the road right now, but I'm working on a new album. We're going to start recording it later this year. It will be my third in just three years."

The awards show was the beginning of a great week in Nashville for Bryan. The following day kicked off the twenty-fifth anniversary of Fan Fair. The week-long festival is held every June and has become an increasingly popular event. People travel from all over the world for a few days of concerts and autograph sessions with their favorite country stars. When Bryan performed at the Asylum Records show that week, the crowd went wild. "We love you, Bryan," they screamed as he sang his string of hits. And the 1996 Fan Fair was also very special for Bryan because it marked his first fan club party. His fan club, which was still fairly new, already had more than twenty thousand members. Four hundred and fifty of his most loyal admirers traveled to Nashville that year just to meet him. His party was held at Nashville's Melrose Lane Bowling Alley, and his fans started lining up early in the morning.

At the party, Bryan was dressed casually in shorts and a T-shirt. He started the day by telling his fans, "Do whatever you want. We'll just be loose today. I know almost each and every one of you from traveling all around the country, so we'll have a lot to catch up on and a lot to talk about. We may even sing a couple of tunes."

Bryan put his excited fans at ease. When one young girl asked him, "What's your middle name?" he replied, "Shelton. But I always wanted it to be Michael, so my initials could be BMW."

Bryan spent the day meeting each one of his fans personally. He tried his hand at bowling but found he was a little rusty. "I used to be really good, but I'm not very good now," he confessed.

To the delight of the crowd, Steve Wariner arrived to lend his support. He joined Bryan onstage for an acoustic concert. Bryan and Steve sang several duets together, including the Beatles' "Get Back." Bryan also gave a miniconcert of his own biggest hits.

Bryan's party lasted until one in the morning. He signed autographs, gave out hugs and kisses, and posed for pictures. "My first fan club party was a huge success." he told a reporter. "Actually, this whole week has been fun. I couldn't be happier."

The one thing that topped his week at Fan Fair in 1996 was the Country Music Association (CMA) Awards. When the nominations for the thirtieth annual CMA Awards were announced, Bryan received two nominations: Best Male Vocalist and the Horizon Award for the Best New Artist.

He was completely surprised by it. "I was fishing on Lake Erie when I heard that I was nominated," he remembers. "I got so excited that I immediately called my mom to tell her. I was honored to be nominated in the Horizon Award category, but I was tickled to be included in the male vocalist category. The other nominees [Vince Gill, Alan Jackson, George Strait, and Collin Raye] have all influenced me."

The star-studded CMA Awards Show was held on October 2, 1996, at the Grand Ole Opry and telecast live on CBS. There was a rumor that

LeAnn Rimes, who had had an incredible first year in the business, might take home the Horizon Award. But when it was time to announce the name of country music's most promising newcomer, the Horizon Award went to Bryan.

It was the highlight of his career. Backstage in the press room, he excitedly said, "Wow, this is a big honor. I never expected this. I honestly didn't think I'd win. I'm just getting over the fact that I was nominated."

The Bryan White express continued to pick up steam throughout 1996. By the end of the year he had sold a combined figure of more than two million copies of his first two albums—an astounding amount in such a short time for a new country artist. His albums were on both the country and pop charts. And they continued to sell phenomenally well.

Not one to rest on his laurels, Bryan went right back into the studio and started working on his third album, *The Right Place*. Recording this album was a turning point for Bryan. He found himself becoming increasingly relaxed in the recording studio. He got involved with every aspect of putting the album together, including writing songs, choosing musicians, and even playing drums on the last track.

"Making this album was a lot of fun," says

Bryan. "I wanted to record the best songs I could and have a good time doing it. I love being in the studio. That's what artistry is for me—being there for every note that's played and sung. I don't understand how someone can go in and put their voice on ten songs and leave. It kills me every second I'm not there."

For the first time, Bryan voiced every creative opinion he had and stuck with it. "I stood my ground with this record," he says. "I didn't let a song go on there that I was iffy about."

The one song Bryan wanted on the release but didn't get was "Imagine That," which he wrote with Derek George. "We all talked about it," says Bryan. "I wanted to record it, but the producers thought it would be better if a band recorded it. It was eventually given to Diamond Rio. They had a number-one hit with it. I'm happy the song found a good home."

Bryan cowrote three songs on *The Right Place*. He wrote most of the material on the road. "A lot of people say it's tough to be focused and creative when you're on the road, because it's a weird setting," he says. "I admit that it's a hard thing to do. But I've written mostly everything that way and I think I've gotten used to it."

The longevity factor in Bryan's career can be linked to the songs he writes or chooses to record.

There's never a throwaway track on his albums. For Bryan, the song is the most important thing. "Songs are born with the writer and they grow up in the studio," he explains. "I'm there with my producers to make the song believable and deep. It is *the* most important thing to me. I am not going to be able to communicate the real meaning of a song if I can't make it believable."

Bryan is a relentless perfectionist who is determined to build a career rather that just score hits. He says he got lucky with the songs he recorded on *The Right Place*. He was most excited to record "One Small Miracle" because it was written by Bryan's idol, Steve Wariner, and Bill Anderson.

"Steve came in and sang on the song and that was a big deal for me," says Bryan, who returned the favor by playing drums on one of Steve's albums. It isn't unusual in Nashville for artists to sing or play instruments on each other's albums. When Steve was working on his instrumental album, *No More Mr. Nice Guy,* he asked Bryan to play drums on a cut called "The Brickyard Boogie." Bryan handled the assignment with earnestness and zeal.

He remembers, "Steve called us up one day and said he wanted us to play on this track. I went in with a couple of guys in my band. But the day before the session I practiced drums so hard that when we went in the studio, my hands were practically bleeding. I had blisters on every finger. I was so serious about it because I didn't want to mess up. It was just incredible. To this day, I can't believe I got to play on a Steve Wariner album." To add to his excitement, Bryan earned a Grammy nomination for "The Brickyard Boogie."

His creative horizons had definitely expanded. His producers, Billy Joe Walker and Kyle Lehning, were aware of it. "His style as an artist has always been extraordinary, but Bryan took his gift to a different level on his third album," says Lehning. "It has been a treat to watch him develop. Every time I get in the studio with him, I'm impressed by what he brings to the table. He's an old soul leading a youthful movement in country music."

As Bryan's album was nearing completion, Asylum Records geared up to launch it with a media blitz the likes of which Nashville had never seen. The marketing campaign included television, radio, and print ads.

The Right Place was released in September 1997. It shipped gold, meaning advance retail sales exceeded five hundred thousand copies. It immediately jumped onto the country radio pop charts.

Bryan feels *The Right Place* recaptures all the excitement of his debut album. "My first album was really cool," he says. "It had a little magic about it because we just tried to make a neat record that would give me an identity. There are a couple of songs on *The Right Place* that take you back to the feeling we had on the first one."

The Right Place begins with the lively "Love Is the Right Place," which was written by Marcus Hummon and Tommy Sims. Bryan decided he wanted to record this song because he related to it. "Lyrically, it's a song that talks about finding your place in the world, where you're the happiest," he says.

The hypnotic "What Did I Do (to Deserve You)" was written by Jamie Houston, Andy Goldmark, and James Dean Hicks. It's a humbling look at the true nature of love. According to Bryan, it's the kind of song that means something different to everyone who hears it. "I love this song," he says. "It has such a strong melody."

"Never Get Around to It," written by Bryan and Derek George, is a riveting look at a guy trying to get through the day without the girl he loves. "We wrote that song in Canada," says

Bryan. "It was right around the ACM Awards. I was flying back and forth to ACM rehearsals. Somewhere in the middle of it, we wrote the song."

Songwriters Skip Ewing and Bob DiPiero penned the heartbreaking "Leave My Heart Out of This." Bryan says, "It's a very sad song about a man who is trying to be honest about his feelings. That part is a lot like me. I'm never going to let anybody go without letting them know what I think. People deserve that from me. We all deserve honesty—especially in a relationship."

The album's next cut is "The Natural Thing," a fun song written by Allyson Taylor and Larry Byrom. "It's a lot like me," says Bryan. "I'm not ready for a serious relationship yet. I'm having too much fun. This song reflects that."

The sleeper cut on the album is the country ballad "One Small Miracle." "That's the most traditional country song I've ever done," says Bryan. "It just blew me away when I first heard it. I've never heard a song written from that point of view. It's so unique and haunting. I just think it's a great song."

The night before Bryan cut "Tree of Hearts," he went to the movies with some friends to see *The Lost World*. At the theater he ran into Skip Ewing, who cowrote "Tree of Hearts" with Don

Sampson. Remembers Bryan, "Skip was sitting a few rows ahead of me and we ended up talking through the whole picture. We walked to the parking lot and Skip said he had just written this song and wanted me to hear it. I told him we were recording the next day, and he said, 'You'll get a tape tomorrow.' He got it there and we cut it. The song tells a great story about everlasting love. It's reminiscent of 'Rebecca Lynn.' Those themes never seem to grow old with people. This is the one that will really get to my grandma."

The compelling "We Could Have Been" has an interesting story behind it. Bryan first heard it on Vince Gill's album *When I Call Your Name*. Pearl River recorded it on their first album. "I always thought it was a great song," says Bryan. "I almost put it on my last album. I'm glad I got the chance to record it. It's slipped through a lot of fingers, but I really made it my own."

Bryan, Derek George, and Bob DiPiero wrote the bouncy "Bad Day to Let You Go" in just one hour. "It was one of those magical days where we sat down and the three of us just clicked," recalls Bryan. "The song has a hip little groove to it that's fun."

The last cut on the album is "Call Me Crazy." Bryan started playing this song in his concerts long before he recorded it. "Every time we played it, fans really responded to it and wanted to hear it again and again," says Bryan, who penned the tune with Derek George and John Tirro. "We wrote this song a long time ago. I wanted to include it on *Between Now and Forever* but it was too late. I'm glad it's on this one."

Bryan called *The Right Place* his most personal album to date. In an interview at the time of its release, he said, "It kind of represents what's happening with me. I'm at a point in my life where everything seems to be falling into place. I have a great family, a lot of great friends, I'm doing what I love to do for a living. I feel very content. That's what this album is all about."

The success of the album put Bryan's name high on the list of the year's most popular stars and secured his place in the world of country music.

seven

live onstage

Seeing Bryan White in concert is an experience unlike any other. From the moment he comes out, the audience feels electricity in the air. His raw, driving energy never stops.

Onstage Bryan knows exactly what he is, an entertainer who will do what it takes to get an audience up on their feet and dancing in the aisles. No other artist has been able to capture all that is exciting about a live performance and to command the stage as consistently as he has.

Bryan's awe-inspiring concerts have played a key role in helping him to develop his mass following. Even before audiences knew who he was, Bryan had the ability to win them over. He started by opening for established country acts. A typical show for him, at that time, consisted of a thirty-minute set, or roughly six songs. Through his determination to pass on a message, Bryan sang his smooth, chilling ballads with an incredible amount of feeling. With an acoustic guitar as his only backup, he made the audiences feel very comfortable. More and more, he found that people were interested in seeing him.

On his twenty-first birthday Bryan played at the Marina Civic Center in Panama City, Florida. It was a memorable night for him. He was the opening act for country singer Tracey Lawrence. When Bryan started his set, he looked out into the audience. With everyone listening to him closely, he decided to say a few words to them. "Hope you guys are good to me, because it's my twenty-first birthday today," he announced, and started to strum his guitar. A few chords later he was surprised with balloons, a red guitar-shaped cake, and "Happy Birthday" being sung by Tracey Lawrence and the entire audience.

As Bryan's popularity started to grow, his shows got bigger and better. But he still took every gig that was offered to him. Bryan's philosophy is that he wants everyone to get the chance to see his shows. That's why he feels it's important to appear at county fairs and festivals all over the United States.

These events are a staple of a country performer's itinerary because they expose the singer to a vast number of record buyers. Sometimes entire towns come out to a fair or festival. After a day of playing games and riding rides, they are treated to a concert by their favorite performers. Bryan has always enjoyed the atmosphere of playing his music in the heartland of America. He also loves seeing parts of the country he's never seen before.

He's made countless appearances at record stores and Wal-Marts across the United States. In 1995, in addition to his regular tour schedule, Bryan agreed to perform in the Wal-Mart Country Music Across America Tour. A large group of up-and-coming country artists participated in these shows, including Deana Carter and Wade Hayes.

Bryan felt that playing the Wal-Mart tour "introduced my music to people who might not ordinarily hear it. We found out we had fans in places we weren't aware of."

After the shows, he signed autographs for hours inside the store. Not only is Bryan a dynamite entertainer onstage, but he does more than required to satisfy his fans offstage. Why does he do it? "I love it," he says. "It's a true pleasure to meet people face-to-face who are responsible for what I do."

Bryan also knows how it feels to be a fan of someone else. "I was influenced by a bunch of artists growing up," he says. "If I met someone I liked and they weren't nice to me, I would have been devastated. I never want that to happen."

After a concert in Cincinnati, Ohio, the crowds for Bryan were so intense, the police broke up his autograph line after just fifteen minutes. What did Bryan do? He made an announcement to the crowd to meet him at his hotel. There he posed for photos and signed autographs for everyone.

At another concert, he walked along a fence where a group of fans were waiting for him. Instead of jumping back into his tour bus after his show, he signed autographs and talked to his fans for another hour.

Did any accidents ever happen during one of Bryan's shows? "Actually, there have been a few mishaps," he says. "One night we were running around the stage so much, we all bumped into each other. Another time I got hit in the hand with a guitar. But no one's ever really gotten hurt. I guess until that happens, we'll just keep doing what we're doing."

There was one show that was simply a nightmare for Bryan to get through. He was scheduled to appear at a small Texas club. At first everything seemed to be going smoothly. At the sound check, all the amplifiers worked and the sound system seemed perfect. The show started right on schedule. As the audience applauded, Bryan kicked off the show with a sizzling version of "Look at Me Now." Suddenly, smack in the middle of the song, the power cut out. Only Derek's amplifier was working, so he kept playing.

Bryan didn't know what to do. As Derek continued to play, Bryan stopped singing and told the audience, "Thank you." He figured he'd wait in the bus until they fixed the problem. But as he was walking off the stage, Bryan thought about the fans who had paid to see him.

"I went back onstage and grabbed my acoustic guitar," says Bryan. "Derek, Brinson, and I sat in the middle of the crowd and played for thirty minutes, until they got the power running again."

When the power was restored, Bryan jumped back up onstage and finished his show. "I almost got through my last song when the power cut out again. But by that time, we were pretty much done. We gave almost a two-hour concert."

Does Bryan ever get stage fright? "Sure, I've had times when I've been really, really nervous," he says. "But I've never freaked out onstage. I think everybody gets a little nervous. I feel nervous before every show. I think it's because I have to talk to the audience. In the beginning I couldn't do that. But now I talk to them as if I was just talking to another person."

The key to the success of Bryan's concerts has been the camaraderie he and the members of his band share onstage and off. Because Bryan has a group of good friends with him on the road, he can relax and be himself. "We're all a unit," he says. "I want the band to be noticed as much onstage as I'm noticed."

When Bryan started going out on bigger tours, the press became more interested in wanting to interview him and review his shows. Bryan hired Holley & Harman, a public relations firm, to handle the requests. But he needed to hire a road manager, someone who would travel with him and keep track of his schedule. He decided to give Brinson Strickland the job.

Besides playing guitar with Bryan onstage, Brinson does double duty organizing all the press requests. Bryan feels totally confident with Brinson as his road manager because he trusts him completely.

In early 1996 Bryan went on tour with Vince Gill. Even though Bryan was not considered a headliner yet, he shared billing with Vince. The fans who came to the shows were excited to see both performers.

Bryan remembers, "I asked Vince if I could sing one of his big hits, 'Liza Jane,' in the show. He said yes, but only if we did it as a duet." The duet became the highlight of the Vince/Bryan shows. Everywhere they played, they got standing ovations.

Like all country-music stars, Bryan travels in a custom tour bus. Bryan's home on wheels is filled with all the things he loves. He has a satellite TV with "millions of channels. You can just sit there and flip channels all day long," he says.

But he prefers playing music to watching TV. "We have the greatest stereo system on the bus. Everybody's got their own collection of CDs that they bring along, and we'll play anything and everything—sometimes till four o'clock in the morning."

Most country stars have two buses on the road: one for themselves and one for the band. Bryan is one of the few headlining acts to ride in the same bus as his band. "We're all so easy to get along with," he says. "I'll always ride with the band. It's more fun. I don't want to have a bus of my own.

That's way too gaudy for me, and I don't like being by myself."

Even though Bryan and his bandmates have loads of fun on the bus, it is strictly G-rated. There is zero tolerance for unruly behavior. Bryan has a list of strict rules that are in force whenever he's on the road. Overnight female guests, drugs, and alcohol are not allowed. The only guests allowed on the bus are family members.

Bryan insists that everyone keep a clear head. "We're crazy enough as it is," he says. "If we drank or did drugs, we just wouldn't be in this business."

Derek George seconds Bryan's notion. He says, "Think of all the singers you saw growing up. If you thought they were taking drugs, you wouldn't have thought nearly as much of them. We've got a chance to be a positive influence. That's what we ought to be."

Every ice chest on Bryan's tour bus is filled with Coca-Cola, Sprite, and spring water. As for food, the refrigerator is filled with mostly cold cuts.

The hardest part of Bryan's job is trying to maintain a good work ethic while maintaining good health. It can be tough sometimes to eat healthy foods on the road. Bryan is adamant about keeping the refrigerator stocked with vegetables. He also keeps a constant supply of cereal on the bus, as well as his favorite snacks: sunflower seeds and Gummi Bears.

Early in Bryan's career, he started to eat Gummi Bears before going onstage to do a show. He found that they gave him energy. He has passed that ritual on to the guys in his band. Now, before every concert, Bryan and the guys consume a handful of Gummi Bears each.

Things have really worked out nicely for Bryan. His Look at Me Now Tour, which played smaller venues, was sold out everywhere. Still, he remains modest about his success.

"To this day, Bryan will look at me on the bus just before we're ready to go onstage and he'll say, 'Think anybody's going to show up?'" says Brinson. "And every show we've done has been sold out. Why does he say it? Because he's the real deal. Bryan is really very talented. It's not a bunch of production. What you get is *him*. He's the most consistent performer I've ever played with."

Continuous touring and singing have certainly sharpened Bryan's vocal skills. He admits, "After being on the road so much, your voice strengthens. It's gone out on me a number of times over the years. But when it comes back, it's stronger."

The only downside to singing every night is that Bryan's voice has changed a bit over time. "I've got a lot more rasp in my throat than I did for the first album," he says. "I wish I didn't have it. I think it's just going to be there because of being on the road so much. I can't do anything about it. Overall, I think I've become a better singer."

eight

double dynamite

bryan White first met LeAnn Rimes when she
was twelve years old. He was playing a New
Year's Eve show at Cowboys in Dallas, Texas,
when he was introduced to LeAnn. He still remembers their first meeting.

"Somebody brought her over to me and said,
'This is LeAnn Rimes. She's a singer, she just
signed with Curb, and she's twelve.' After my
jaw dropped, I said, 'She's twelve?' The first
thing I told her—and she remembers this, too—
was to just have fun. I told her not to grow up too
fast."

It was the beginning of a lasting friendship between Bryan and LeAnn. After their first meeting, LeAnn's career took off like a rocket following the success of her debut album, *Blue*. She met a lot of people along the way, but she never lost contact with Bryan.

"I think we really relate to each other well," says Bryan. "When LeAnn gets tired of dealing with something and being around everybody, she calls me up to get away from all that stuff. She's one of my best friends."

In 1997 fans fueled a rumor that Bryan and LeAnn were more than just friends. After LeAnn was spotted in the audience at one of Bryan's Fan Fair shows, the tabloids reported she had a huge crush on him. The rumor floating around the gossip grapevine was that country's hot young stars were secretly dating.

The truth behind this rumor is that Bryan and LeAnn are just good friends who support each other's careers. Whenever LeAnn has some extra time, she loves going to see her favorite stars in concert. Bryan feels the same way. When it came time to invite another performer to appear with him at his fan club party, he asked LeAnn to be his special guest.

In June 1997 Bryan participated in a lot of

different events at Fan Fair. His second fan club party was held at a roller-skating rink in Nashville. He got the day started by answering questions from his audience. Then he gave a rocking concert. Before beginning his autograph session, he sprang a surprise on the crowd. "I'd like to introduce you to my friend LeAnn Rimes," he said. They sang Bonnie Raitt's "I Can't Make You Love Me," and cleared up the romance rumors.

By this time Bryan and LeAnn had a pretty good idea that they would be touring together the following year. Their performance at Bryan's private party was a warm-up. So was their appearance at CountryFest '97, where they teamed up for another surprise duet.

"Over the years we talked about touring together," says Bryan. "But our schedules always conflicted. We looked far ahead and said the only way this is going to work is if we stop now and decide we're going to do it. We prepared for it for about eight months."

The news of their tour leaked out to the press months before it began. Anticipation for a show starring two of country music's biggest and brightest stars was very high. Fans of both stars couldn't wait to see them live.

Bryan and LeAnn spent weeks putting their

Singer Shelby Lynne congratulates Bryan on winning the American Country Music Top New Male Vocalist Award. *(Copyright © 1996 by Connie Ives/Hot Shot Photos)*

Handsome and talented, Bryan has taken the music world by storm and captured the hearts of fans around the world. *(Copyright © 1997 by Bob Ives/Hot Shot Photos)*

"There's nothing that can match the feeling I have after I get off the stage," says Bryan. "The concerts are the ultimate for me!"
(Copyright © 1996 by Bob Ives/Hot Shot Photos)

One of the highlights of Bryan's career was winning the Country Music Association Horizon Award in 1996.
(Copyright © 1996 by Bob Ives/Hot Shot Photos)

Bryan performs with Glen Campbell. *(Copyright © 1996 by Alan L. Mayor)*

Bryan with his best friend and songwriting partner, Derek George. *(Copyright © 1996 by Alan L. Mayor)*

Author Grace Catalano (left) and her mother, Rosemarie Catalano, met Bryan backstage after a concert. He gave Grace an exclusive, in-depth interview. *(Copyright © 1998 by Rojo Entertainment)*

Bryan looked terrific as he accepted his award as 1996 Male Star of Tomorrow at the TNN/Music City News Country Awards show. *(Copyright © 1998 by Rojo Entertainment)*

Actress Jennifer Love Hewitt with Bryan at the 1998 American Music Awards. *(Copyright © 1998 by Bob Ives/Hot Shot Photos)*

In concert, Bryan thrills fans with his electrifying stage presence and awesome vocal range. *(Copyright © 1998 by Bob Ives/Hot Shot Photos)*

Bryan and his girlfriend, actress Erika Page, step out for a night on the town. *(Copyright © 1998 by Connie Ives/Hot Shot Photos)*

Two of country's hottest stars: Bryan White and Tim McGraw. *(Copyright © 1996 by Connie Ives/Hot Shot Photos)*

Bryan compares musical notes with country singers Neal McCoy (left) and Paul Brandt (right). *(Copyright © 1996 by Connie Ives/Hot Shot Photos)*

Bryan and LeAnn Rimes love performing together. *(Copyright © 1998 by Karl Roberts)*

Bryan and his father, Bud White. *(Copyright © 1998 by Karl Roberts)*

Bryan loves the outdoors. *(Copyright © 1998 by Karl Roberts)*

show together and rehearsing it. "There was a lot of rehearsing," says Bryan. "Days on end of rehearsing. But I wanted it to be the best it could be."

They named the tour after the Bonnie Raitt song "Something to Talk About," and it officially kicked off in New Orleans at the UNO Lakefront Arena on Thursday, January 22, 1998. Bryan and LeAnn performed separate shows and then sang two songs together for the finale. Their show was a huge hit. Audiences and critics loved it. *USA Today* gave their show three stars. They said of Bryan, "White set the tone for the concert. He paced his set quickly and worked the crowd."

The tour marked Bryan's first outing as a headline performer playing in large arenas. Headlining a tour was a whole new experience for him. "It's a lot of weight on your shoulders," he says. "But all of that is so challenging to me. The stage set is probably the largest set that we've ever put together. There's not a lot of theatrics with us. We wanted it to be a real musical-based show."

In Bryan's set, he sang everything from Stevie Wonder's classic "Signed, Sealed, Delivered I'm Yours" to the theme from the old TV series *The Jeffersons*. Surrounded by his band, Bryan energized the show. He greeted the audience with a big "Hello! Are you ready to have a party?" He moved in perpetual motion back and forth across the stage, so everyone could get a chance to see him. Guitar in hand, he soared through hits like "So Much for Pretending," "Someone Else's Star," and "Love Is the Right Place." Then for his encore, he showcased his talents on the drums while he sang the Diamond Rio hit "Imagine That," which he'd cowritten.

With the amount of energy that he has onstage, it's amazing that Bryan doesn't warm up before a show. "I don't do anything special," he says. "I just hang with the band. I like to get a vibe happening before I go out there, and then I'm ready."

Bryan says his tour with LeAnn was "the best show that I've put together so far. It was real versatile and it covered a wide spectrum of music. We set out wanting people to come to the show not knowing what to expect, and I think we succeeded."

LeAnn also had some surprises in store for her fans. She performed most of her hits, but she also threw in covers ranging from Patsy Montana ("I Want to Be a Cowboy's Sweetheart") to Prince ("Purple Rain") to Aerosmith ("Cryin' ").

Bryan and LeAnn crossed musical boundaries in the rousing finale. They returned to the stage to perform Ben E. King's "Stand by Me" and Bonnie Raitt's "Something to Talk About." In the finale Bryan took complete charge—clowning with LeAnn and leading her by the hand while they sang. The fun they had onstage was so infectious, it put a smile on the face of every concertgoer.

Early in the tour Bryan said, "Don't expect the same show every night. The beginning of a tour is never like the end. By the end, we eliminate all the stuff we get bored with."

Bryan and LeAnn decided to add a song to their finale because they wanted to be onstage together a little longer. In addition to "Stand by Me" and "Something to Talk About," they added "From This Moment On," which Bryan had recorded with Shania Twain.

Bryan loved this part of the show. "The coolest reaction from the crowd always came at the end, when we were singing together," he says. "That got everybody really excited, because *we* were really excited. LeAnn and I worked really well together. I think everyone who saw our show went away feeling happy and entertained."

Many fans wanted to know when Bryan and

LeAnn would record their own duet. "I'd love for us to do a duet," says Bryan. "We're going to. I just don't know when. It's been a kind of a conflict-of-label type of thing. It has nothing to do with us. If it was up to us, we'd have it done by now. But we're going to do one sometime soon. We kick around three or four different songs every time we see each other."

In the meantime, while he was waiting to cut a track with LeAnn, he recorded a duet with Shania Twain. The superb "From This Moment On" is on Shania's album *Come On Over,* and Bryan was honored to sing it with her. Shania chose Bryan because "he's the best male voice in country music."

How did the pairing of Bryan and Shania come about? It all started with a phone call. Brinson Strickland walked onto Bryan's bus one day and told him that Robert John "Mutt" Lange (Shania's husband and producer) was on the phone. Bryan remembers, "I grabbed the phone and it really was Mutt Lange. He told me he was writing a new song with Shania and they wanted me to sing it with her. My first reaction was 'Yes, when do I need to be there?' "

Bryan flew to New York and spent a few days with Shania and Mutt at their house upstate. "I sang my part of the song, rode horses, and just soaked up input," says Bryan. "They let me do exactly what I wanted to do. I think we blended real well together."

When Bryan arrived at Shania's house, she had already recorded her part of the song. "Vocally, it was very challenging. It was so different from anything I had ever done," says Bryan. "I'd never actually collaborated, as far as a duet, with anybody before."

Bryan says Shania and Mutt are two of the nicest people he's ever met. "Shania's just great," he says. "I think sometimes her talent gets overlooked because of her looks. She really is an artist who is not only a great singer, but someone who's not afraid to take a chance and be creative. I think it's really cool of her to step out and do what she wants to do."

Bryan was equally happy to be working with Mutt Lange, a successful producer and songwriter who worked with stars like Bryan Adams and Michael Bolton. "I was really freaked out at the opportunity to go watch Mutt Lange work in the studio," Bryan says. "He's the epitome of what I think a producer should be. He's unbelievably talented. And he's great to talk to. He has such respect for everyone."

Now that Bryan's had the chance to tour with LeAnn and has cut a duet with Shania, is there any other country gal he'd like to work with? "Yes," he says with a grin. "I've always loved Martina McBride. I think it would be neat to work with her, too."

nine

one small miracle

The date was April 19, 1995. It was the worst day of Bryan's life. He was on his way to Wichita Falls, Texas, for a concert when he heard the devastating news: the Alfred P. Murrah Federal Building in Oklahoma City had been bombed. With his family all living in the area, Bryan froze for a minute. Then he panicked.

The first thing he did was reach for the phone, but he couldn't get through. All the lines were busy; no one was able to get through. The tragedy hit Bryan hard. He knew his grandfather often did business inside the Murrah Building.

Bryan learned later that his grandfather was almost one of the victims. "My grandpa, who is an auctioneer and owns an antique store, actually did have an appointment down in the Murrah Building the morning of the bombing," says Bryan. "A last-second business call changed his plans. If he hadn't gotten a phone call and, in a split second, made the decision to go a few minutes later, he would have been inside—and he'd be gone."

Bryan's grandfather, Wilford, explains, "I called the Social Security office the afternoon before, because I needed to fill out some paperwork. They told me I couldn't get it done before they closed and suggested I come in at nine the next morning. But that morning a man called and asked to see an antique, so I decided to go to the Social Security office later—and that office was one of the worst hit."

Bryan's grandmother, Shelley, was at home when the explosion occurred. Bryan's grandparents live just five miles from the city. "I was combing my hair," says Shelley, "when the mirror started shaking and some windows broke. I thought it was an earthquake."

Bryan was clearly shaken by the bombing and wanted to do something to help the victims' families. But he had to wait. His publicist at Asylum Records called him the day it happened and asked if he was interested in doing a charity event that could raise money for the children affected by the bombing.

"I was immediately interested in helping any way I could, but I didn't want to make a publicity stunt out of it," says Bryan. "That would make me kind of fidgety. I don't think the dust will ever settle down on that, but after enough time went by, it calmed down. When I felt like it was time, we all started doing something. We thought there were a lot of kids left without parents and what better thing to do for them than raise a scholarship fund to pay for their schooling."

Because the tragedy hit so close to home, Bryan put together not one but two charity events to help Oklahoma City heal. On August 10 Bryan and some of his Nashville friends held a benefit concert and silent auction at Nashville's Wildhorse Saloon. The money they raised was given to the Federal Employee Education and Assistance Fund (FEEA). It will ensure that all children who lost parents in the bombing will get an education.

Bryan asked country, sports, and Hollywood stars if they would donate an item that could be auctioned off. Everyone wanted to help. Some of the items Bryan received included a *Pulp Fiction* movie poster autographed by John Travolta, a cowboy hat autographed by Gene Autry, a leather saddle belonging to Randy Travis, Joe Diffie's electric guitar, and a basketball signed by Magic Johnson.

But the biggest surprise came from country star Alan Jackson, who donated his beloved white 1965 Mustang convertible to the auction. Bryan couldn't believe Alan's generosity. "We asked him for a cowboy hat and some boots," says Bryan. "He said he couldn't find them. Then he asked, 'How about a car?' I was speechless. That car is worth a lot of money, but even more than that, Alan's cars mean so much to him. I was flattered and thankful that Alan was so supportive."

At the auction, Bryan's grandfather was the auctioneer. Bryan and his brother kept track of the bids. The auction was a big success.

A few months later Bryan decided it was time to go where the tragedy happened and stage another benefit concert. He visited the site of the bombing on October 1, 1996, the day before he won the CMA Horizon Award.

When Bryan arrived in the city, he was overcome with sadness. "I was so moved when I saw all those symbols of love on the fence surrounding the bomb site that I couldn't even talk," he says. "I walked around not saying anything because I just couldn't put my sadness into words."

Bryan was silent as he lingered by a sign that read: "We came here to remember those who were killed, those who survived and those changed forever. May this memorial offer comfort, strength, peace, hope and serenity."

Bryan also visited Heartland Chapel, a wooden building built immediately after the bombing, where survivors and their families went for solace. "Being on the site made the tragedy even more real," he says. "Actually standing where it happened. I felt sadness for those killed, and hurt and anger because someone did such a terrible thing."

At night he put on an invitation-only benefit concert for the victims' families at the Oklahoma Opry. The ninety-minute concert was part of a fund-raiser that aired on ninety-three radio stations.

After his show Bryan stayed at the Opry until 2 A.M. so he could meet all the children. When he met Krista Genzer, whose mother died in the explosion, Bryan's eyes filled with tears. Krista told him that because of his help, she would be able to fulfill her dream of becoming a nurse.

"That night was a very emotional night," says

Bryan. "It hit me harder than I thought it would." He raised more than $75,000, but he continues to help the kids in Oklahoma. He recently turned his energy toward raising money for a memorial to be built on the site of the explosion. Bryan is genuinely concerned about how those children who lost their parents will cope in the years ahead. "That's something that's going to affect them for the rest of their lives," he says. "I'm still trying to do whatever little I can to help them out."

The work he did to help the children of the Oklahoma City bombing did not go unnoticed. He was invited to the annual federal employees' gala dinner in Washington, D.C. He also received the Country Radio Music Humanitarian Award for his dedicated and unstinting efforts. "I don't want anyone to forget about what happened in Oklahoma City," he says. "The more people know about it, the more they will donate their time and money to helping those kids."

Bryan also lends his time generously to a host of other charity events. He is very modest about his success; he isn't the type to take his celebrity status too seriously. Instead he uses his popularity to help others. Whenever the opportunity arises, Bryan is ready to lend his support to any worthwhile cause.

"I've been asked to be involved with many different causes," Bryan reflects. "Sometimes we have to turn some down, but I've tried to participate in most of them. It's important to me."

Some of the events give Bryan a chance to have fun while he's helping others. He races cars in the annual Mark Collie Celebrity Race for Diabetes Cure and plays basketball in Vince Gill's annual celebrity basketball game and concert, which raises money for Belmont University's athletic and music-business programs.

At the eighth annual game Bryan told reporters, "I played eighth- and ninth-grade basketball and sat on the bench. I always tell everybody this is my chance to redeem myself from those years. Maybe I'll get to play tonight."

Bryan did get to play, and he played well, but he lost a shoe as he ran down the court. When he saw it was missing, he looked at the crowd, laughed, and hastily kicked the other one off. His antic was the highlight of the game.

Bryan is dedicated to helping people in need. He is truly one of the most caring guys in the music business. "I think of how fortunate I've been in this business," he says. "I like to know that I'm giving something back."

ten

the dating game

"**i** want what everybody wants: a family, a wife and kids," says Bryan. "But right now there isn't time for it."

Even though Bryan has little time for romance, he loves having a girlfriend to share things with. In a recent interview he was asked what he'd been doing when he was ten years old. He answered with a big smile, "Most likely I was chasing girls."

The first girl who turned Bryan's head was in his second-grade class. "Her name was Angela and I was in love with her," he says with a smile.

For weeks he tried to get up the nerve to talk to her. Finally he decided he'd break the ice by buying Angela a present. He remembers the day he tried to give it to her. It was one of his most embarrassing moments.

"I bought her this heart-shaped necklace and wanted to give it to her after school, " he recalls. "I had my mom pick me up and follow Angela home. I got out of the car about a half block behind her. I walked up to her and tapped her on the shoulder. She swung her purse around and knocked me on the ground. My mom was laughing and Angela was laughing. I never gave her the necklace. To this day, I think she really liked me, but I don't know."

Bryan has always been aware of the kind of girl he is looking for. He knows she must be levelheaded, sincere, and understanding. The girl for Bryan has to be able to handle all the pressures of his business. She needs to accept his busy schedule and appreciate his need to put his work first.

Bryan is an affectionate guy who constantly shows his feelings. He needs someone who will share his interests and support his career. He likes to be around someone with a good sense of humor. He's constantly cracking jokes and loves having a good time. When Bryan dates someone he devotes himself to that person; otherwise he would feel very selfish.

Since he's found fame, he's been on several dates. One girl he dated for a while was Emily Bradley. They were spotted arm in arm at many events. When he won the CMA Horizon Award, Bryan leaned over and kissed Emily before walking up to the stage to accept his trophy. After that night Bryan's career heated up, and he found himself touring more than ever to support his albums. It put a strain on his relationship with Emily, and they broke up.

Bryan admits that with his busy schedule, it's difficult to have a personal life. He works around the clock. When he isn't writing songs or recording, he's touring or attending charity events.

He says that being labeled a heartthrob hasn't helped him in the love department. "Actually, I think it makes it more difficult for me to meet someone," he said in an interview. "A lot of girls catch my eye all the time, but I haven't caught up with the right one yet."

Then he met Erika Page, a pretty, dark-haired actress best known for her work on the soap opera *The Bold and the Beautiful* and the TV series *Second Noah*; she is currently working on *One Life to Live*. When Bryan began dating Erika, he found that she possessed many of the qualities he had been searching for.

Because she is an actress, she understands the business Bryan is in. Erika has seen Bryan's career rise to the top and is not jealous of the mail he receives or the fans who chase after him. She knows it's all part of show business. Erika is as well adjusted as Bryan, and the two make a stunning couple.

When Bryan first started taking Erika with him to awards shows, he was amazed at the number of photos the paparazzi took of the couple. "At one show they asked us to pose and then chased us all the way in," says Bryan.

The only problem they have had is that they are maintaining a long-distance relationship: Bryan lives in Tennessee and Erika lives in New York. But they manage to spend a lot of quality time together. So far it's been working. Bryan says their relationship is filled with "mutual respect and lots of space."

As their relationship has grown stronger, everyone has been wondering if Erika is the girl who will take Bryan out of circulation.

Well, during the end-of-1998 holidays, the world got its answer. Bryan took the actress to Rockefeller Center and presented her with a four-carat engagement ring, which Erika happily accepted. So "the most eligible bachelor in country music" may be romantically off the market, but his fans can still look forward to seeing Bryan perform and hearing his great, cool voice!

eleven

you know how i feel

In addition to his thriving music career, Bryan
has joined the ranks of singers who have ven-
tured into acting. As a kid, he used to stand in
front of the mirror and recite lines from his favorite movies. But he is quick to point out that he
never thought about going into acting.

That is, not until the producers of the soap
opera *The Bold and the Beautiful* called Bryan's
management office. It was October 1996. Bradley Bell, executive producer and head writer of
the show, needed a hot country artist to introduce a new story line. "We wanted to add a club
to the set," says Bell. "We decided to make it

country because the world has such a fascination with the American dream, and country music is as mainstream Americana as it gets."

Bell wanted Bryan to appear on the soap for a week to kick off the opening of the show's fictitious Canyon Country Club.

"When they asked me to be on it, I asked if they knew I'd never acted before," says Bryan. "They said they'd write a part that fit me. So I said I'd do it. My immediate concern was that I wanted to do a good job."

Bryan was nervous when he got to the set, but the cast and crew members quickly put him at ease. While he was in the makeup chair, Bobbie Eakes, who plays Macy, gave him some acting tips. Director Nancy Eckels explained that she might ask him to repeat his lines several times for additional camera angles.

Bryan appeared on the show over three days. He had four short scenes with dialogue and performed "So Much for Pretending." As he waited for the cameras to roll, he calmed himself down by playing his guitar. "Once I began getting into the act, it started to be fun," he says. "I was playing myself, although it wasn't really like me."

In one scene, veteran actress Phyllis Diller cut in front of Bryan's autograph line to flirt with him. The embarrassment on his face was real. "I couldn't help it," he says. "It was the first time I've ever done anything like that. But it was a big honor to do a scene with Phyllis Diller."

Bryan's first acting stint turned out to be a positive experience for him. Even though it was a bit nerve-wracking, he has toyed with the idea of doing more acting. "I may take acting classes to get a feel for things," he says. "But I will only do it again if I feel completely comfortable about it."

So far, the only other acting project Bryan has gotten involved with was the animated feature film *Quest for Camelot*. He did the singing for the lead character, Garrett. The character's speaking voice is supplied by Cary Elwes. Bryan says, "I was tickled to be part of *Quest for Camelot*. I couldn't believe it when they told me David Foster suggested me for the singing part. He's a great producer and songwriter." Foster cowrote the film's songs with Carole Bayer Sager. Bryan sings "I Stand All Alone," and does the duet "Looking Through Your Eyes" with Andrea Corr, who is the singing voice for the female lead character, Kayley.

Bryan enjoyed working on *Quest for Camelot*. "It was different because I had to lose my Oklahoma accent and sound almost British," he says. "They put the camera on me while I was recording the songs. When they did the animation, the character of Garrett has the same expressions I had while I was singing."

Bryan has been working so hard over the past few years, he rarely has a day to call his own. The constant work sometimes takes a toll on him. There are times when he looks exhausted. He blames it on the fact that he doesn't get enough sleep the night before he has to perform on an awards show or do a TV talk show. "Sometimes I stay up all night because I'm excited and also worried about an appearance," he says. "Some people have actually come up to me and said, 'Boy, you look so tired.' But I'm used to it. Now, it's almost like a compliment."

Bryan also suffers from allergies. When allergy season hits, his eyes and his voice are affected. To keep his voice strong before singing, he drinks a lot of water and tries not to talk. When his eyes start to look puffy from allergies, his remedy is to apply cold spoons or cucumber slices, which he says "really works."

Bryan is very conscious about looking his absolute best at all times. The one thing he often worries about is the way his hair looks. He spends a lot of time styling his hair, trying to get it to look good. "I have to keep washing and blow-drying it," he says. "In high school, I'd put in all this mousse, and it would end up looking so bad,

I'd have to wash it again and go to class with a ball cap on."

Bryan constantly changes his hairstyle. When he first moved to Nashville he wore a shoulder-length ponytail. He admits now, "I didn't have a good sense of style." He trimmed off the ponytail but kept the hair long. When his second album was released, he cut his hair short and changed the color to a darker shade of brown. "I could probably guarantee you that in a year I won't have the same hairstyle. I like change," he says. "I like the unexpected. I think that's my motto: the unexpected."

In early 1997 Bryan unexpectedly decided to change residences. He moved out of the three-bedroom, two-bath house he'd bought in 1996. It came as a surprise to some of his friends because Bryan had completely renovated the house, soundproofing a rec room to serve as a recording studio and putting in new hardwood floors and a new kitchen. But the house, on Lealand Lane in the Green Hills section of Nashville, was not big enough for Bryan.

"I just realized I needed more space," he says. He bought a bigger home in the upscale community of Brentwood, Tennessee, south of Nashville. "The new house is forty-two hundred square feet and has four bedrooms," says Bryan.

"I built a studio below the house, which I think I worried about more than the house itself. The way I see it is upstairs is a place to sleep, downstairs is where I'll spend all my time."

Because Bryan plans to record his future albums in his home recording studio, he installed the best equipment. "A lot of people work on digital," he explains. "That's just a trend. I'm a big fan of analog. I just love the sound of it. So I put in a thirty-two-track analog studio in my house."

Bryan enjoys a quiet lifestyle when he's away from the spotlight. He likes to stay home and work in his studio. He puts on comfy clothes, like faded Levi's and a T-shirt.

He relaxes by going to the movies. "I try to see every movie that comes out," he says. His all-time favorite movie is *Somewhere in Time,* which stars his favorite actress, Jane Seymour. "It's just a great love story, a wonderful movie about undying love," he says.

Today Bryan is a seasoned professional loved by millions of fans. Yet he admits he is a fan himself of many great actors and musicians. When he comes face-to-face with one of his favorites, he will often introduce himself and express his admiration.

On a trip to Los Angeles in 1995, a friend at his management company took him for a drive in the country. Bryan remembers, "I didn't know where we were going until I saw all these stagecoaches." They were out in Agoura Hills, on the set of *Dr. Quinn, Medicine Woman,* the television series that starred Jane Seymour.

"I was stunned," says Bryan. "I couldn't believe it. Immediately my heart was going nuts. I've had a crush on Jane Seymour since I was thirteen. When I met her, I told her I've been a fan since I was a kid. She was so nice and she is one of the most beautiful women on the planet."

Bryan also got the chance to go on a special VIP tour around the set of the soap opera *General Hospital.* When he was growing up, Bryan remembers, his mom had the soap on every day. She was a huge fan. The *General Hospital* stars loved meeting Bryan, especially Brad Maule, who moonlights as a country singer. Bryan was given a specially autographed script by the cast, and Brad dedicated it to Bryan's mom.

Bryan admits that he isn't a big fan of TV because he's usually onstage performing during the prime-time hours. But he does have a favorite show. "The one show I loved as a kid was *The Honeymooners.* That show was hilarious," he says. "And Jackie Gleason was absolutely fantastic."

When Bryan isn't working, one of his favorite things to do is take a long drive. For his first three years in Nashville, he continued to drive his grandfather's old Plymouth Horizon around town. In 1995 he bought a brand-new blue Ford Ranger and decided to return the Plymouth.

Bryan remembers, "My dad came to Nashville to help me put Grandpa's car on a trailer. Then we drove it back to Oklahoma. But somewhere in Arkansas the car rolled off the trailer. While we were trying to get it back on, a family stopped to help us. There were these kids in the backseat. They kept staring at me and finally asked, 'Are you Bryan White?' I said, 'Yes, I am.' And they asked for my autograph. At the same time, their dad was helping us with the car." Bryan gave the kids his autograph. He was so grateful for the roadside help, he invited the family to his concert the following night. Bryan is definitely a hero with a heart of gold.

What are Bryan's favorite hobbies? The two things at the top of his list are golfing and fishing. He loves fishing so much that he says if he weren't a singer, he'd be a professional fisherman. "I always wanted to be on a fishing show," he says. "My dad used to tell me, 'You know, son, the music business is great, and if you're successful, that's terrific. But if you can get on a fishing show, you've pretty much made it big.'"

Bryan got his wish when he appeared on the

TV show *Fishing Country,* which is filmed in north Texas. The show's host, champion bass fisherman Charlie Pack, climbed into a boat with Bryan and Carly Jarmon, the 1996 Miss Texas. They cast their lines into the water and, in less than one minute, Bryan reeled in a one-and-a-half-pound bass. He held it up for the cameras, then released it into the pond. Bryan caught and released fifteen bass that day. After the show, Charlie Pack said, "Bryan is a great fisherman. You can tell he's fished a lot."

Bryan was introduced to fishing when he was ten. "My grandfather and father used to take me fishing all the time," he says. "I was thirteen when I really started to like it. I don't get to fish a lot now because I'm always working. But I'd like to do it every day. Fishing gives me peace of mind."

Once in an interview Bryan was asked what his idea of the perfect day would be. He remembers, "I said I'd go fishing and eat sunflower seeds and drink tons of Coca-Cola. Right after that, I started to get bags and bags of sunflower seeds from fans. I've learned you have to be careful what you ask for, because you just may get it!"

Bryan can't deny the fact that life has certainly changed for him, but he wouldn't have it any other way. He's one of the hottest stars in music, and he's enjoying every minute of it!

twelve

looking ahead

bryan's success has been staggering, yet he has managed to keep it all in perspective. He credits his family and close friends for keeping him well grounded. "My friends don't have stars in their eyes when I see them," he admits. "They treat me like they treated me when I was in high school. Just the same, normal me, which is really cool."

Even though Bryan is a local celebrity back home, music has remained the family business for his parents and his brother.

Bryan's mom, Anita, is a favorite Oklahoma club singer who only recently retired. "I don't know why she retired so young," says Bryan. "She's a great singer and needs to keep singing."

His dad, Bud, now lives in West Palm Beach, Florida, where he sings with his second wife in a duo called Easy Street. Bryan's younger brother, Daniel, is also planning a career in music. He plays the sax and drums in a Christian rock band called Ninth Hour.

A lifelong dream of Bryan's is to record a song or two with his family. He already included his mom in the choir on a song he recorded for the compilation album *Amazing Grace II: A Country Salute to Gospel*.

"I was given free rein to really be creative on that album, so I went out and had fun with it," says Bryan. "Because it was a gospel project, I decided to put together three of my favorite gospel songs into a medley. I recorded 'Will the Circle Be Unbroken,' 'I'll Fly Away,' and 'Jesus Loves Me.' That's how the choir came together and why it's so unique. I invited my band, some friends, and my mom to be in the choir.

"That was fun for Mom, but I still have plans in the future to really feature her on a song instead of just putting her in a group," Bryan continues. "I want to get Mom and Dad to play and sing on a record that actually gets released to radio."

Bryan has etched his mark into country-music history with a youthful, fun, distinctively different, and energetic style. From the moment he released his first album, he's been on a rocket ride to the top.

So where does this multiplatinum artist go from here? As far as his music is concerned, Bryan continues to have surprises up his sleeve. A lively concert performer, he works to keep his concerts fresh and new. "We change around the arrangements to songs so they sound different. That keeps *us* entertained as well as the audience," he says.

His fans will be pleased to know that Bryan wrote a great deal of new material for his fourth album. He collaborated with different songwriters, including Richard Marx, and recorded the majority of the tracks in his home recording studio.

"I know it surprises a lot of people that Richard Marx is writing songs in Nashville. But he's a really great melodic and lyric writer," says Bryan. "I think his forte has always been a lot of great ballads. He had a lot of success with songs like 'Right Here Waiting' and 'Hold On to the Nights.' "

Bryan continues to find all music exciting. He loves listening to R&B and soul music. His favorite is Stevie Wonder. "His stuff is some of the best music ever recorded, especially the songs on his unbelievable album *Songs in the Key of Life*," says Bryan. "There's so much truth to it, and I think it doesn't fall into any category. It's just great music. Country-wise, it's still Steve Wariner and Vince Gill for me. But I realize that there's a lot of other great music out there, too."

Even though Bryan enjoys listening to all kinds of music, his heart remains in country. "If I were to go anywhere else with my music, I'd be betraying something about myself," he explains. "This is where I belong."

Bryan is one of the fastest-rising and most successful young artists in country music. He's had an amazing number of hit singles. His concerts are consistently sold out. And he's a major winner of awards.

What is the secret of his success? A big factor is that Bryan takes things day by day rather than setting long-term goals. "I've always been that way. If I get caught up in goals, I think I would forget what's going on right now in the present."

Part of Bryan's appeal is that he has remained unaffected by his sudden burst of success. His fans refer to him as "one of us." Bryan is still the casual, unassuming, shy guy from Oklahoma whose heart belongs to his music above anything else. He has not given in to trends or fallen victim to fame. Bryan has remained honest with himself and with his fans. He possesses a unique ability to create music that touches the hearts of people everywhere.

What does the future hold for Bryan? Plenty—new albums, a Christmas album, more concerts, perhaps a TV or movie role. The sky's the limit for Bryan White. He has achieved unlimited success in country music and will continue to do so in the years ahead.

"My accomplishments are far from over," he says. Then he adds with a smile, "I just don't see how life could get any better. I have everything I want right now!"

BRYAN'S FACT FILE

Full real name: Bryan Shelton White

Birth date: February 17, 1974

Birthplace: Lawton, Oklahoma

Height: 5'9"

Weight: 150 lbs.

Family: Dad, Bud; mom, Anita; younger brother, Daniel

Hair: Brown

Eyes: Hazel

Current residence: Brentwood, Tennessee

Favorite amusement park ride: The Texas Giant at Six Flags over Texas

Favorite actor: Harrison Ford

Favorite actress: Jane Seymour

Favorite movie: *Somewhere in Time*

Favorite song of his own: "Look at Me Now"

Favorite holiday: Christmas

Favorite Christmas carol: "The First Noel"

Favorite performers and influences: Steve Wariner, Vince Gill, Charlie Rich, Merle Haggard, John Conlee, Ronnie Milsap, Stevie Wonder

Favorite hobbies: Going to the movies, playing his music, and recording in his home studio

Favorite color: Forest green

Favorite sports: Fishing, golf, basketball

Favorite food: Mexican

Least favorite food: Meat loaf

Favorite snacks: Sunflower seeds, Gummi Bears

Favorite clothes: T-shirt and jeans

Biggest thrill: Hearing his voice on the radio the first time

Instruments played: Drums, guitar

Car: Blue Ford Ranger

Ideal girl: "I'm attracted to a girl who is a genuinely nice person."

Idea of a fun date: "Going to the movies and dinner. Or maybe just talking somewhere quiet so we get to know each other."

Education: Graduated from Putnam City West High School in 1992

Early bands: Christian rock band, jazz band

Arrived in Nashville: October 1, 1992, in his grandfather's old Plymouth Horizon

Previous jobs: Songwriter for Glen Campbell Music; T-shirt vendor for country group Pearl River; busboy at the High Noon Saloon

Movie appearance: *Quest for Camelot* (Warner Brothers, 1998). In this animated movie, Bryan provided the singing voice for the lead character, Garrett.

TV appearances: *The Bold and the Beautiful; TNN/New Year's Eve Live at Sea World in Orlando, Florida; Alien Vacation* (Sea World special); *Fishing Country; Kathie Lee Gifford Christmas Special; Christian Country Awards* (host)

Secret desire: "I hope through my music, I'm able to add some fun to people's lives."

Personal ambition: "Stay as happy as I am right now!"

Professional ambition: "I want to continue to grow in all I do as an artist, a songwriter, and a performer."

BRYAN SPEAKS OUT

on singing

"Even when I was eighteen and leaving for Nashville, I knew all I ever wanted to do was sing. I never sat back and thought about what I had to fall back on if this didn't work. I disregarded that whole idea."

on songwriting

"I think I've been progressively getting better at writing. I'm stronger in certain areas, like melody and ideas. But Derek's [Derek George, his guitarist and songwriting partner] a really good lyricist, so we work well together."

on his number-one hit song, "rebecca lynn"

"I loved that song way before I got the chance to record it. It was on one of Skip Ewing's albums. He cowrote the song. I used to play his version of the song every morning over and over again. I was so lucky that I got the chance to record it."

on being satisfied

"I'm never one hundred percent satisfied. I don't think I ever will be. That's what keeps me reaching. But I am at a place where I'm very content."

on his concerts

"It's great when you hear people singing along and clapping and cheering. It makes your job onstage that much easier because you know the audience is in your corner."

on his personality

"I'm never real stern about anything. I'm always pretty laid-back. I know there's a point where you have to act like a grown-up, but I'm having too much fun to feel like a grown-up right now."

on his music

"I'm learning every day. I want to grow with each record and keep things fresh. I'm not trying to go over the same territory twice, but I also don't want to be radically different. On my first album, the ballads were the big hits. On the second one, the faster ones were popular. The singles off the third CD were both slow and fast. I like my listeners to be entertained with a variety of music."

on playing the grand ole opry

"When you play the Grand Ole Opry, you start thinking about the history of the place and the vibe of being in the same place where so many legends performed. I love playing the Opry because they treat you like family."

on his favorite christmas gift

"Other than all the cool stuff my family has given me over the years, I think my favorite gift came from Steve Wariner and his wife, Caryn. One day Caryn asked me what my favorite Steve Wariner song was. I told her I loved a song he wrote called 'Our Savior Is Born.' When Christmas rolled around, they presented me with a frame. Caryn had framed all Steve's rough drafts of the song when he was writing it, different versions of it, with things written all over pieces of notebook paper. That isn't something I can go out and buy. It was a real neat gift."

on overnight success

"There's a risk in overnight success in that you might go straight to the top and then right back down. People might not take you that seriously. You might become a novelty to them because of that. I don't think I've been so much an overnight success. I feel like I've had a stepping-stone type of career. It seems like each year and with each record things get bigger and better."

on playing clubs

"As a teenager, I played clubs with my parents. The whole club experience actually molded me for what I'm doing now. When we travel out to these clubs whenever I'm out on the road, I feel like I've already been in some of these places before."

on his worst fear

"My worst fear is something bad being said about me that is not true. I treat everybody exactly the way I want to be treated."

on his fans

"I'll be somewhere and these girls will be yelling, 'Oh, Bryan! Oh, Bryan!' and my band will be around me laughing. It's funny in a way, but it's real cool, too."

on his future

"Over the years I've learned more about the recording studio and engineering and the whole production end of things. I love producing. I probably will produce in the future."

DISCOGRAPHY

bryan white
(Asylum Records, released October 1994)
Produced by Billy Joe Walker, Jr., and Kyle Lehning

Tracks
"Eugene You Genius"
(Lonnie Wilson/Billy Lawson)

"You Know How I Feel"
(Bryan White/Derek George/Jim Weatherly)

"This Town"
(Greg Barnhill/Jan Buckingham)

"Someone Else's Star"
(Skip Ewing/Jim Weatherly)

"Look at Me Now"
(Bryan White/Derek George/John Tirro)

"Rebecca Lynn"
(Don Sampson/Skip Ewing)

"Me and the Moon"
(John Tirro/Sam Gay)

"Nothing Less than Love"
(Wayne Tester/Rusty Young)

"Going, Going, Gone"
(Bob DiPiero/John Scott Sherill/Steve Cropper)

"Helpless Heart"
(Paul Brady)

Recorded at Nightingale Studio and The Sound
Emporium in Nashville

bryan white—
between now and forever
(Asylum Records, released March 1996)
Produced by Billy Joe Walker, Jr., and Kyle Lehning

Tracks
"Sittin' On Go"
(Josh Leo/Rick Bowles)

"Still Life"
(Mac McAnally)

"Blindhearted"
(Bryan White/Randy Goodrum)

"Nickel in the Well"
(Chris Waters/Lonnie Wilson)

"I'm Not Supposed to Love You Anymore"
(Skip Ewing/Donny Kees)

"So Much for Pretending"
(Bryan White/Derek George/John Tirro)

"Between Now and Forever"
(Bryan White/Don Pfrimmer/George Teren)

"A Hundred and One"
(Rich Wayland/Kye Fleming/Mary Ann
Kennedy)

"On Any Given Night"
(Bryan White/Allison Mellon/Jeff Ross)

"That's Another Song"
(John Paul Daniel/Monty Powell/Doug
Pincock/Jule Medders)

Recorded at Nightingale Studio and Woodland
Studios in Nashville

bryan white—the right place

(Asylum Records, released September 1997)
Produced by Billy Joe Walker, Jr., and Kyle Lehning

Tracks

"Love Is the Right Place"
(Tommy Sims/Marcus Hummon)

"What Did I Do (to Deserve You)"
Jamie Houston/Andy Goldmark/James Dean
Hicks

"Never Get Around to It"
(Bryan White/Derek George)

"Leave My Heart Out of This"
(Skip Ewing/Bob DiPiero)

"The Natural Thing"
(Allyson Taylor/Larry Byrom)

"One Small Miracle"
(Bill Anderson/Steve Wariner)

"Tree of Hearts"
(Skip Ewing/Don Sampson)

"We Could Have Been"
(Don Cook/John Jarvis)

"Bad Day to Let You Go"
(Bryan White/Derek George/Bob DiPiero)

"Call Me Crazy"
(Bryan White/Derek George/John Tirro)

Recorded at Emerald Sound Studios, Woodland Studios, and Seventeen Grand in Nashville

appearances on other albums

The Best of Country Sings the Best of Disney
(Walt Disney Records, 1995)
Bryan sang "When You Wish Upon a Star"

Amazing Grace II: A Country Salute to Gospel
(Sparrow Records, 1995)
Bryan sang "Will the Circle Be Unbroken/I'll Fly Away/Jesus Loves Me" medley

Froggy's Country Songbook
(Virginia Records, 1996)
Bryan narrated the story of "Jack and the Beanstalk"

Steve Wariner—No More Mr. Nice Guy
(Arista Records, 1996)

Bryan played the drums on the instrumental "Brickyard Boogie" with Steve Wariner, Derek George, Bryan Austin, and Jeffrey Steele

For Our Children, Too
(Rhino Records, 1996)
Bryan sang "You Are My Sunshine"

Traveller (Soundtrack)
(Asylum Records, 1997)
Bryan sang "Rockin' Robin"

Shania Twain—Come On Over
(Mercury Records, 1997)
Bryan and Shania sang the duet "From This Moment On"

Quest for Camelot (Soundtrack)
(Curb Records/Warner Sunset Records/Atlantic Records, 1998)
Bryan sang "I Stand All Alone"
Bryan and Andrea Corr sang "Looking Through Your Eyes"

AWARDS

ACADEMY OF COUNTRY MUSIC
Top New Male Vocalist, 1996

COUNTRY MUSIC ASSOCIATION
Horizon Award, 1996
SRO Touring Artist of the Year, 1996

TNN/MUSIC CITY NEWS COUNTRY AWARDS
Male Star of Tomorrow, 1996

ENTERTAINMENT RADIO NETWORKS
COUNTRY RADIO MUSIC AWARDS
Best New Artist, 1996
Single of the Year, "Rebecca Lynn," 1996
Humanitarian Award, 1997

COUNTRY WEEKLY MAGAZINE
Golden Pick Favorite Male Newcomer, 1996

WHERE TO WRITE
TO BRYAN

**Do you want to send Bryan a letter?
Here are some handy addresses:**

Bryan White International Fan Club
P.O. Box 120162
Nashville, TN 37212

Bryan White
c/o Asylum Records
1906 Acklen Avenue
Nashville, TN 37212

Bryan White
c/o GC Management
1114 17th Avenue S. #102
Nashville, TN 37212

The official Bryan White Web site is at:
www.bryanswhite.com

ABOUT THE AUTHOR

Grace Catalano is the author of four *New York Times* bestsellers: *Leonardo DiCaprio: Modern-Day Romeo, Leonardo: A Scrapbook in Words and Pictures, New Kids on the Block,* and *New Kids on the Block Scrapbook.* Her other books include biographies of LeAnn Rimes, Brad Pitt, Joey Lawrence, Jason Priestley, Paula Abdul, Gloria Estefan, Richard Grieco, Fred Savage, River Phoenix, Alyssa Milano, and Kirk Cameron. She is also the author of *Meet the Stars of* Dawson's Creek and *Teen Star Yearbook.* Grace Catalano has edited numerous magazines, including *Rock Legend, Star Legend, The Movie Times, Country-Beat, Country Style,* and the teen magazine *Dream Guys.* She and her brother, Joseph, wrote and designed *Elvis: A Tenth Anniversary Tribute, Elvis and Priscilla,* and *Country Music's Hottest Stars.* Grace Catalano lives on Long Island's North Shore.